How to

MARRY RIGHT AND AVOID DIVORCE

How to
MARRY RIGHT AND AVOID DIVORCE

*Tips from Thirty-Three Years
of Private Practice*

SUSANA K. O'HARA, PH.D.

TATE PUBLISHING *& Enterprises*

Published by Tate Publishing & Enterprises, LLC
127 E. Trade Center Terrace | Mustang, Oklahoma 73064 USA
1.888.361.9473 | www.tatepublishing.com

Tate Publishing is committed to excellence in the publishing industry. The company reflects the philosophy established by the founders, based on Psalm 68:11,
"The Lord gave the word and great was the company of those who published it."

Book design copyright © 2011 by Tate Publishing, LLC. All rights reserved.
Cover design by Lauran Levy
Interior design by Joel Uber

Published in the United States of America

ISBN: 978-1-61739-943-5
1. Family & Relationships; Marriage
2. Self-Help; General
11.03.01

In memory of my mother,
Nati Horvath Krivatsy (1925–2009)

ACKNOWLEDGMENTS

For preliminary reviews of parts of the manuscript, I would like to thank my fellow practicing psychologists Carolyn J. Smith, Ph.D. and Ann Flynn, Ph.D. Both made excellent suggestions concerning general aspects of this work.

For repeated, thorough review of the manuscript as it evolved through its many forms, I am grateful for the advice of my three adult children Tom, Christina, and Bill. I am fortunate that all three are good, disciplined writers and knowledgeable in the ways of today's world. Their efforts ensured that the manuscript is readable by the general public.

For contributing acceptance and rejection criteria to be used in choosing a partner for marriage, I am indebted to the many good people I interviewed. Several mental health professionals and clergy contributed criteria they felt were important for a stable and happy marriage. These criteria are located in Appendix A. Readers are welcome to use them.

For exacting input from a man's point of view and for endless hours of assistance, I am thankful to my husband, Tom. Without his skilled contributions, this book may not have seen the light of day. Although he sometimes might have preferred to be on the golf course instead of in my office, he needs to remember that he caused this book to be written when he worked overseas for six months, thereby providing me with lots of spare time to write this book.

For teaching me how to listen and other counseling skills, I want to thank my one-time mentor, now deceased, Thomas M. Magoon, Ph.D.

For the gift of using these skills over the years, I want to thank all my clients.

TABLE OF CONTENTS

Part Two

Part One

Do you wonder if you can find someone to marry and have a fulfilling relationship for the rest of your life? Are you thinking of getting married but wonder how to find that right person? If so, keep reading. I wrote this book to help you marry well.

I want to emphasize that happy, stable marriages do exist. One of the best rewards in life is the companionship and comfort that a good marriage provides. I believe that most people can have a good marriage if they are disciplined and careful about whom they marry.

So how can you marry the right way? How can you find the person you will be compatible and happy with?

Through my work as a psychologist for thirty-three years, I have identified some of the major steps that people can take to marry right. In addition, I have lots of personal experience as well, having been married for thirty-five years myself. In this book, I share the knowledge I gained through these years of professional and personal experience. In general, people will marry well if they do the following:

- Avoid believing in myths about marriage and think realistically

- Decide what is important in life

- Decide, before emotional involvement, what kind of a person they will accept or reject based on well-defined criteria

- Become experienced at meeting and evaluating people, especially with regard to important personality characteristics detailed in chapter two

- Be self-disciplined, make self-improvements as advised, check out information, and accept guidance from trusted people.

Does this take effort? Yes. However, your efforts should yield results. Many people followed these steps, got married, and report that their marriage is going well.

In part one of this book I explain the steps in detail and show how you can follow them. Part two contains examples of how real people worked on their problems in psychotherapy, moved forward, and succeeded in marrying well. Some of these people were already once or twice divorced when they came to therapy, but once in therapy, they focused on how to marry well the next time.

If you worry about becoming a divorced person once you marry, I want to emphasize that for people who marry right, the divorce rate is actually quite low. It is much less than the 50 percent rate advertised by the media. In chapter two I describe some of the research on divorce to show you what I mean.

By following the suggestions in this book, I believe you can avoid becoming a divorce statistic. Even better, you will improve your chances of having a happy and stable marriage.

I

⟡⟡⟡

A Case Study and a Discussion of Common Myths

Nothing is more dangerous than wrong ideas—
because ideas have consequences.

Thomas F. O'Hara

If you choose the wrong man or woman to marry, you will have problems. Chances are you'll divorce. If you don't, you'll continue in an unhappy marriage. I wrote this book to help you avoid both. Every word of this book is written to help you avoid the collateral damage of an unhappy marriage and divorce.

It is my experience that many marriages fail because people believe romanticized, unrealistic, and wrong ideas about love and marriage. These ideas exist because people simplify and glorify the notion of love. I call these wrong ideas "myths." Myths lead to poor choices in dating and marriage, which I see when people come to me and pour out their sorrows and hurts. I am starting this book by describing some common myths because I have seen how myths lead people to making poor marital choices.

One Role of Psychotherapy:
Helping People Identify Their Myths

Every case is different. Many times therapy starts with a crying, angry, and distraught person who needs to mourn a failed relationship. Besides the sorrow, there is anger at being hurt and upset with oneself for having made a bad choice. Many clients blame themselves for making choices they should not have made. What was my client thinking of when she decided to marry someone she knew to be a heavy drinker? Why did my client decide to marry a woman he knew had serious emotional problems?

Many marriages I have seen were destined for failure from the beginning. My clients believed in myths about love and marriage and made bad choices. Their mythical thinking wove a fantasy about the other person. Only after marriage and a series of disappointments did my clients realize that the people they married were not the people they thought they were.

One of my roles as therapist is to help clients understand the myths they believed in that caused a failed relationship or marriage. Therapy is a process. Once the client understands, I assist the client in replacing myths with self-selected, well-thought-out, core value screening criteria. These criteria are unique to each person, and I will discuss how to develop them. The final step is to apply the criteria in real life to real people. With the application of the criteria, the client is much more likely in the future to select a spouse with whom he or she will have a good marriage. Generally speaking, this is what happens when a client decides to follow the steps and ideas I describe in this book.

The following is from the case study notes of my upset client Karen. Her belief in a myth led to her disastrous second marriage.

Love at First Sight:
Why Karen Married Stu

The root cause of Karen's marital problems was traced to her belief in the myth of "love at first sight." Her belief in this myth led to a quick marriage to Stu. The price tag of her haste and infatuation? Unlimited and unforeseen problems, including violence. You will note, as I uncover the depths of this marriage, that more and more problems surface. Karen never knew the real Stu until after she married him.

One November morning, an elegantly dressed businesswoman turned heads in my waiting room when she arrived for consultation. At age forty, Karen had been married to her second husband, Stu, for about a year. The trouble was that her marriage was falling apart. Her face and body were tense with worry and frustration.

"My husband is usually a nice, happy person," Karen began. "At least I thought he was. But what he did upsets me so much. I don't know who I am married to anymore."

Karen's old cocker spaniel had cancer. The dog was like a child to Karen, who was childless. Karen and Stu agreed that the dog would be put to sleep at a time they decided together. The agreement also included that they would have a child as soon as possible.

When Karen went to sleep one night, her dog was wagging its tail. Two hours later Stu woke Karen out of a deep sleep. He was yelling that the dog had relieved himself on the carpet, so he shot the dog in the head with his shotgun. Then he threw the dog into the fire pit in the backyard.

"I never had a chance to say good-bye to my dog." Karen's agony shook my office. "He is such a jerk! He was drinking again. He never lived up to the contract."

"What contract?" I wondered, deciding to delay the issue of the shotgun in the hands of a drunken man.

"The contract to control his drinking!" Karen shouted; then she started to cry. Through her sobbing, she said, "We went to see a marriage counselor last summer. We went because Stu got drunk and threw my cell phone through a window. I was scared and insisted that we talk to a counselor. Stu was apologetic and said everything would change. He said I would never have to be afraid of him again. He made a contract with me to cut back on his drinking. But he hasn't changed."

While Karen was crying, I was thinking. There had been two acts of violence within six months (one with a weapon) and the couple had been married only a year? This did not sound good. Was this just the tip of the iceberg? Maybe. I needed more information.

"Karen, did Stu ever act like this before? You know, violently?"

Karen took a minute to collect herself. Then she thought for a while. I saw her shoulders sag inside the immaculate business suit, as though she were collapsing into herself.

"Well, yes, now that you mention it," she said in a hollow voice. "Last winter, shortly after we married, Stu got drunk and we fought. I told him I wanted him to stop drinking. He got really mad and took off on the snowmobile."

"How was that violent?"

"There was no snow on the ground."

Stu had churned up the ground of neighborhood properties and ruined the snowmobile. Although embarrassed by Stu's behavior, Karen did not feel afraid of him at the time. She even called the neighbors to make apologies.

That made three acts of alcohol-driven rage in the first year of marriage. Karen was right to worry. What was really going on here?

I asked Karen about the history of her relationship with Stu.

"My family lives out of state," Karen explained, "and I was married before to a very violent man. I only saw him as a charming man at first; the violence came after we married. He said it was my fault, and I believed him. He said it was my fault due to my success in business. My success overshadowed his. Anyway, we divorced. Then I met Stu, and I thought I hit the gold mine. He was funny, nice, and successful. Both of us being successful in business, I thought it would work. I knew from the first that I wanted him. We were engaged four months after we met and married within the year. He told me he drank every now and then, but I never saw the rage until after we married."

Karen started crying again. "At first I thought Stu's heavier drinking was my fault. I thought maybe I just drove men to drink. But I talked to Stu's sister and mother, who said Stu had needed to stop drinking for a long time. So I know this time it cannot be my fault."

For a smart businesswoman, how can Karen be so naïve? I wondered to myself. Instead I said, "Karen, the drinking is the fault of the person who is drinking, no matter who they blame for it. It is always the fault of the person who is drinking, okay?"

I saw her nod in agreement, so I continued. "Now, what did Stu's mom and sister mean that Stu had needed to stop drinking for a long time?"

Karen's eyes were focused on the pattern of my office rug.

"I don't know. I asked, but they said nothing. They seemed uncomfortable."

Because the therapy session was drawing to its end, I had to get back to the gun issue. As a therapist, my primary concern is for the wellbeing and safety of my clients. It is my duty to warn a client of any danger he or she may be in. Stu's drinking pattern and the use of the shotgun while he was drunk presented a clear danger to Karen. I asked Karen where Stu kept the shotgun. Karen said Stu told her he had burned it in the pit with the dog's carcass. I replied that the gun needed to be found and emphasized that she could be in danger herself. I instructed Karen to find the gun and give it to a trusted family member or the police. Stu was too dangerous to have access to any kind of weapon.

In the following therapy visits, Karen had a lot to report. Stu told Karen that the gun he had killed her dog with was not a shotgun but a BB gun, which he burned in the pit, along with the cocker spaniel.

Karen's report troubled me for two reasons, which I recorded in my notes.

First, while I do not know much about guns, I do know a little something. I know that the pellet from a BB gun is not likely to kill a cocker spaniel because it lacks sufficient velocity to penetrate into the animal. The pellet itself is too small. Maybe twenty pellets in the same location of the dog's head would kill it, but Stu, in his drunken rage, would not be able to shoot so accurately. On the other hand, a blast from a shotgun would definitely do the job. So was Stu lying about the type of gun he used? I thought it likely.

Second, Stu said he had burned the gun in the pit. If that were the case, there would have been some trace of the gun left, after the fire went out. Guns are built of materials tempered to withstand high temperatures. The gun would not turn to ashes and should still be visible in the pit.

I listen for inconsistencies (as well as consistent information) in what clients report. To me it sounded like Karen was naïve about men, alcohol abuse, and weapons. I thought it probable that Stu knew this and capitalized on her lack of knowledge. So was he changing the gun story to protect himself? Is that why it was a BB gun now instead of a shotgun?

Despite searching the house from top to bottom, Karen found no gun. Maybe it was in the pit, like Stu said. Then at least the barrel of the weapon would be found, I told her. Had she looked into the pit? No, she said, because she couldn't stand to see the remains of her beloved dog. I was willing to bet Stu knew that.

While I was thinking, Karen was saying that she and Stu had had a heart-to-heart talk in which he confided that many years ago he used to drink and get into fights. He said he was much better now because he didn't fight anymore.

"Doctor, there was a pattern of drinking and violence before he married me. I also found out something else very upsetting."

What else could there be to this potentially dangerous and agonizing marriage? As it turned out, on her own initiative, Karen confided in her brother-in-law, who happened to be a police officer.

The officer did some research and informed Karen that Stu had a DUI traffic violation two years before she met him. During their recent intimate conversation when Stu appeared to be truthfully discussing his drinking and fighting history, he neglected to mention this recently-obtained DUI. Karen was stunned when her brother-in-law told her about it. Stu was still withholding information. She hung her head.

"Doctor, I don't need you to tell me that I was fooled again. The person I thought was a gold mine is a really sick man. I know I can't trust him anymore. But how come I was fooled two times? How can I trust myself to make any decisions when it comes to men?"

Good, I thought. *Karen is ready to listen.*

I talked about myths and how people believe in them. I talked to her about how people marry based on these myths. In her case, her immediate attraction to Stu led to a quick decision that he was the one for her. Within a few weeks of meeting him, Karen thought her search for a mate was over. She was delighted when Stu proposed marriage.

Karen never once questioned Stu's motives and never asked herself the following important questions:

- He has not even met my family yet. What is his rush to marry me?

- Do I really know him well enough?

- I have been divorced once already. Shouldn't I take more time to get to know him better, just to make sure that I am not making another mistake?

Karen should have checked out Stu's background before she ever went out with him. Had she done so, she would have found the negatives, which were now forcefully, painfully unfolding before her. By this time, there was plenty of information to diagnose an enduring pattern of alcohol dependence and alcohol-related violence. I emphasized to Karen how serious this was and the type of clinical treatment it required to change it. Karen said she understood.

"I am not going to let it happen a third time. The third time I am going to get it right, or I will not marry again."

But Karen was still in danger because Stu still drank and had access to a weapon. I needed to warn her about safety one more time.

"Karen, I am still concerned about the gun that Stu allegedly used to shoot your dog. As I said before, Stu should not have access to a weapon of any kind. I really am concerned for your safety. You told me that you believe that gun is out of the house, but it should be found. If you can't look in the burning pit in your backyard, could your brother-in-law do it for you?"

Karen agreed. The shotgun (not a BB gun) was found in the woods behind their home. An officer took possession of it.

Karen tried to save her marriage. She asked Stu to enter treatment for alcohol dependence, but he chose to move out of the house and continue drinking instead. Karen lost hope. With a sad and heavy heart, she called her attorney.

The marriage ended, but Karen continued in therapy. With time Karen learned:

- She needed to discard her belief in the myth "love at first sight."

- She needed to learn that love and trust are earned over time.

- She needed to develop and follow clear ideas on what she wanted in a spouse.

- She needed a process to check out if what she knew about a man was true. She had to make sure that what she observed to be the characteristics and personality of the person she was attracted to were real. She needed to conduct background checks and have trusted family and friends give her feedback on the men she dated.

- She needed to remember the simple phrase "Trust, but verify." Always.

Discussion of Several Common Myths

The first task in marrying right is to get your own thinking and priorities in order. Do not choose a spouse based on mythical thinking like Karen did.

People make mistakes even when they think they have good ideas about whom they should marry. They know they should marry someone loyal, attentive, loving, healthy, smart, and from a nice family. Despite this, their mythical thinking can lead them to choose quite the opposite.

Over the years, I have made a list of the most common myths that led my clients to make mistakes. I hope you avoid them.

Myth #1: Love at First Sight

This is the myth that led to Karen's troubles. Love at first sight? What is that first physical attraction? People have described it many ways. Everyone agrees that, first and foremost, it is visual. It occurs before anything important is known about the person. The visual attraction is already there before your brain kicks into gear or before you think of what to say. The visual attraction triggers sexual and chemical attraction, sending butterflies to the stomach.

Of course, the attraction is more than visual and physical. The eyes and brain take in other pleasing cues as well. For example, the attractive gentleman across the hall is not just pleasant of face and body; he also appears relaxed and happy. The good-looking woman who just entered the elevator with you is not only excitingly attractive; she has a bubbly personality. You feel yourself lighting up in her presence, even though you haven't a clue as to who she is. And the distinguished-looking man at the restaurant has a certain confidence about him and is wearing a lovely sweater. When he looks and smiles, you want to smile back. Somehow, he makes you feel special.

Your chemistry does not need any more information to be aroused. The brain (if undisciplined) quickly follows your chemistry with the pleasurable thought of, *Could this be the person for me? Oh, I hope so!*

"Is this the person for me?" How absurd! Stop! Think! You know nothing about the person! How can this be the person for you?

Let's look at it another way. People know how to present themselves to advantage. Do you ever think of people as magicians who do their magic tricks to misdirect and amaze you? Some people are masters of misdirection. How about those attractive strangers? If you looked beyond the appearances and the magical feelings they bring up in you, you would see the real person.

If you knew the real facts, there would be more for your brain to consider. But how could you know (at first glance) that the relaxed and happy gentleman just got out of jail, that the good-looking woman has been married three times already, or that the man in the great sweater has five concurrent lawsuits against him? You do not know any of that at first, which leaves your excited biochemistry unencumbered with such troubling information. It is usually in the absence of information and rational thought that your biochemistry is free to operate. That is when you are most vulnerable to believing the myth of "love at first sight."

Can honesty, loyalty, respect, and other desired characteristics be evaluated at first sight? On first meeting? Definitely not. It takes a long time to truly get to know someone.

This is the myth Karen believed in that led her to two divorces. The way to overcome this myth is to take time to get to know the people you are attracted to. Make it a point to take this time and get your brain thinking. Take lots of time to find out what a person is like and whether he or she is the kind of person you should marry. Do not let anyone rush you into engagement or marriage.

Myth #2: Love Conquers All

The meaning of *love* is different for each person, so it can mean many things: a physical attraction, an emotional connection, a feeling of wanting to help, admiration of personal traits, a hope for financial gain, political alliance, or social connection. Whatever you think love means, imagine you are married to someone who:

- Gambles or drinks away your income

- Abandons you and the children

- Stays out late and cheats

- Does not respect you or care about your emotional needs

- Will not work or is unable to keep a job

If you believe that love conquers these situations, you are fooling yourself. The reality is that love does not and cannot conquer all. If you are abused or neglected, your feeling of love will turn to sadness, disappointment, and hate. People overwhelmed by these feelings want relief and seek divorce. Researchers have shown that love is not enough to keep a marriage going.[1]

In my experience, the one exception is couples that have been faithful and respectful to each other during long-term marriages. They can develop a love that conquers all. This love is a deep attachment built over many years. This love carries a couple through life's trials of illnesses, deaths, disappointments, affairs, military deployments, financial setbacks, and so forth. This type of love is the one you want in your marriage. To attain this love is why you want to marry wisely and well.

Myth #3: If We Live Together before Marriage, Our Marriage Has a Better Chance of Working

Nowadays many people believe that if they live together before marriage, they will know more about each other and that way decrease the likelihood of divorcing. However, research from multiple sources disproves this myth.[2] Cohabitation before marriage does *not* increase the likelihood that your marriage will work. There are three major reasons for this.

First, people who agree to cohabit instead of marry often have less of a moral foundation than people who chose the legal and moral commitment of marriage. People who cohabit have already overstepped an important moral boundary. People who overstep boundaries are less desirable as marriage partners. This is because if they overstep one important boundary, they are more likely to overstep others in the future, such as keeping promises, staying faithful and being responsible. When they overstep other boundaries—however they do it—they can ruin the trust that the marriage is built upon and the marriage itself. If there are children involved, the parents' behavior often damages the moral underpinnings of the children in the family.

Second, living together is different from marriage. Marriage is a union of legal commitment, meant to last forever. Because of that commitment, married people tend to relax and be themselves. Cohabitation is different; it is a union of convenience. In cohabitation, people tend to be on good behavior. Usually one or both of the cohabitants is trying to obtain an advantage from the arrangement. Therefore, they want to make the cohabitation work and act according to what they think the other person wants them to be, although that is not who they really are. Because cohabitation and marriage are so different, living together before marriage does not lead to a better marriage.

Third, people who cohabit may be a select group who are less emotionally mature and have less ability to commit to marriage. Research shows that people who live with several partners before marriage are more likely to have marital problems once they do marry than people who do not live with someone prior to marriage.[3]

Research studies pinpoint one important exception to cohabitation not leading to a good marriage. Couples who are already engaged and planning a wedding when they decide to cohabit are different from those who have no such plan. The couples with firm wedding plans have just as good a chance of staying together after marriage as couples that do not live together before marriage.[4]

Myth #4: There Is Only One Girl/Guy in the World for Me

Many people believe that the person they love is the only person in the world for them. This particular myth is attractive to people who are:

- too young or inexperienced to know any better

- crave simple ideas and the false security of them

- do not have the confidence to believe that someone else could love them

- do not understand human nature.

This myth is one of the most frequent topics in my sessions. To discredit this myth, I explain that most human beings are loving, social creatures, interested in connecting with other people. Because of this, we can love and be loved by many people during a lifetime. That is one reason we have to be careful to pick the right person to marry.

"How is it possible that I could love many people?" is a frequent question. It is possible because most humans are born with the capacity to love, which is an emotional need to be connected to someone else in a meaningful, stable, and committed way. The reason that we can love many people during our lifetime is because we carry the capacity to love inside of us wherever we go. This capacity to love does not change. What changes is the object of our love. Depending on where we go and whom we meet, we find different people to love (and to love us back). That is why you can love several people during your lifetime, or even two people at the same time.

Young, inexperienced people who believe there is only one girl/guy in the world for them rush into commitments. They feel that once they find a person to love, the next thing is to marry them. Love is all they think about; they do not stop to consider if they are truly suited to each other.

Falling in love is one thing. Making a no-divorce marriage is another. For a marriage to work, the situation needs to be right. A person's situation and emotional maturity are the best indicators of when they ought to marry. Generally speaking, the situation is right for marriage when a person:

- Is mature enough to stay faithful

- Has been in and out of love and learned from the experiences

- Has accomplished things they set out to do (finish school, travel, get the job they want)

- Wants a stable, meaningful relationship

- Has thought through screening criteria for a spouse

- Is ready for the responsibilities of marriage and a family

When these qualities are present in both parties, the marriage will likely succeed. Once married, there really should be only one man or woman in the world for you.

Myth #5: We Love Each Other, So We Would Never Hurt Each Other

This myth is widespread because people crave emotional security. Belief in this myth allows people to relax and feel secure, which is perhaps the strongest of emotional needs. Emotionally needy people want to believe that the words "I love you" are all-inclusive and binding by the person who spoke them.

In reality, there is no relationship without some hurt in it. When people marry, their brains and emotions do not get fused together. They continue to think and feel differently. These differences can result in hurt and pain.

If you believe this myth (or any other one), there is a danger zone in your thinking. The danger zone is created when you relax with your "We love each other" guarantee and expect smooth sailing in your relationship. By believing the myth, there is a tendency to be less attentive to the other person. You forget to be considerate and respectful because your belief in this myth gives a false sense of security, so you start taking someone for granted. That is when you are likely to start having relationship problems.

In discussing this myth with clients, I often use the analogy of having money in the bank. I use this comparison because most people can relate to or at least understand this concept.

"The emotional ties you have with each other," I'll say to a couple, "is like a bank savings account.

"Here's how it works. If you make a little investment into your marital savings account, it yields you interest in your marriage. When you make an effort to be kind, your effort is mentally recorded in the relationship account (in your loved one's mind), just as it would be on a bank statement. Then the other person feels he or she wants to reciprocate and also put money in the account. This leads to even more interest in your joint account. With time, effort, and patience, you both grow your account and make it substantial."

A spoken "I love you" by itself is not going to be enough. If you want the relationship account to grow, the words need to be accompanied by acts of kindness and considerate behavior.

Once clients understand this concept, the myth is broken. People understand that their frequent acts of kindness and consideration, not their mythical thinking, make their marriage secure and comfortable.

Investments in the marriage also diminish the pain of hurt. The pain of the hurt is the debit column of a bank account, where money is withdrawn from the account. There is no marriage without some hurt in it, but if the frequent acts of kindness (the deposits) overwhelm the hurtful times (the withdrawals/ debits), people are able to forgive each other, stay married, and live to enjoy happier days (fuller bank savings accounts).

Myth #6: Everyone Marries for Love

Think again if you believe this one! The world is full of people who like being in love but who would never marry just because of it. A person may love you well enough but decide to not marry you. You yourself may have loved someone you would never marry.

Why do people marry if not for love? Over the years, people gave me many reasons that reflect the person's values, strengths, shortcomings, and expectations of their future spouses. I have heard people say they got married because they: believed in one of the myths we just discussed; wanted children right away; got pregnant and believed that marrying was the right thing to do; were tired of living alone or with parents or friends; worried that no one else would ever want to marry them; were convinced by parents and friends to marry; believed it would look better (to the boss, in the eyes of others, etc.) if they were married; wanted to marry an American citizen to live in the United States; thought they would gain social, financial or political advancement by marriage; could not make it financially by living alone, all of their friends were already married, etc.

Are any of these good reasons for getting married?

Not if you want a good marriage. Not if you want a no-divorce marriage.

So, what are good reasons for getting married?

As I mentioned before, the best reason is because you are prepared for marriage and want to marry. You had your single life, did things you wanted to do, learned from your experiences, and now are ready to settle down. You have carefully considered whom you should marry and found a person worthy of marrying.

You are ready to marry if you *do not believe* that marriage is for love only or that love will conquer all of your problems or that there is only one person in the world for you.

When this is your situation and you find a good match, your marriage is likely to work out.

Now, prepare to do some more thinking. In the next chapter I review some of the divorce research and advise you on how to set up your acceptance and rejection criteria for the person you might marry.

2

THINKING—THE FIRST STEP IN MARRYING WELL

I keep a close watch on this heart of mine,
I keep my eyes wide open all the time.

Johnny Cash

The quote above is from "I Walk the Line" by Johnny Cash, which beautifully summarizes what I am urging you to do. The purpose of this chapter is to help you maintain a degree of objectivity (eyes wide open) as you think about selecting a spouse. You should also know the truth about divorce statistics and the characteristics of people who are less likely to divorce.

Keeping your eyes wide open (trust but verify via background checks) will help you avoid myths. Keeping a close watch over you heart will keep you from entering bad relationships. You can accomplish this by getting in the habit of thinking for yourself. In this chapter, I discuss several ideas to help you think objectively as you search for a spouse. I ask you to focus your thinking on the following:

- Identify desirable characteristics in another person that would contribute to happiness and stability.

- Take the time to think and decide on the attributes and characteristics of another person *you think* would be compatible with you. (Do your thinking when you are not in love so your thinking is as free of bias as possible.).

- Based on your thinking, decide upon acceptance and rejection screening criteria for a potential spouse. By selecting these criteria you sharpen and refine your thinking about the kind of person you feel you would be happily married to for a long time. This type of thinking (and follow-through on it) can save you the type of trouble and agony that characterizes failed marriages.

- Apply your screening criteria as you meet people. These criteria are more than just a yes or no checklist for your future spouse. They are also safeguards meant to keep you from relapsing into mythical thinking.

What You Should Know About the Divorce Rate

A fundamental step in your thinking is understanding the research on divorce rates. In particular, you need to understand what types of people are more likely to get divorced. Note that the divorce rate is low among certain types of people. Use this information to your advantage in making up your screening criteria.

Many people assume there is a 50-percent chance that their marriage will end in divorce. They believe the 50-percent divorce rate because that is what they hear on television and from supposedly knowledgeable sources. It is too bad that this statistic is so widespread, because it is incorrect.

The misinformation about the 50-percent divorce rate started a few decades ago, when in one year there were 2.4 million marriages and 1.2 million divorces recorded in the United States.[5]

Someone divided 1.2 by 2.4, and got .5, which is 50 percent. This incorrect analysis is what the media publicized and is accepted by the general public.

The numbers were used incorrectly, and this simplistic calculation should never have been performed. What is correct is that in 1981 there were 54 million marriages already in existence, which the statistics did not take into account. The divorce rate should have been estimated by contrasting the 1.2 million divorces with the 54 million marriages already in existence, and not with the 2.4 million marriages that occurred in the one year.

The divorce rate is a difficult statistic to properly calculate. As such, you should be skeptical about divorce statistics. Indeed, when I looked for a more accurate, current statistic, I was not able to get one. The reason is that in 1996 the National Center for Health Statistics stopped collecting detailed, yearly, state-by-state statistics on marriage and divorce. From 1997 on, more than 80 percent of all Americans were completing the short form of the US Census, which no longer asks about marital status.[6] As of 1997, there have been no nation-wide divorce statistics collected.

Thus we have no exact count or any accurate national estimate as to what today's divorce rate is. All we have are estimates of the divorce rate by various researchers who research small samples of people and then from that group of people make estimates of the divorce rate for the whole population.

That is why social researchers come up with different estimates. For example, one estimate is that only 11 or 12 percent of marriages end in divorce.[7] Another researcher put the figure at a 34 percent estimate.[8] Other studies suggest that the rate may be on the order of 41 percent.[9] Again, the reason for this variation is that researchers use small and different samples of people to estimate the divorce rate for the US population. Depending on the groups of people used in the research sample, the researchers get different results.

Keeping Your Chances of a Divorce at a Minimum

Whatever the divorce rate is, it is too high. The eyes-wide-open process of selecting screening criteria is designed so you decrease your chances of becoming a divorce statistic yourself. You need to understand two things in this section:

1. The characteristics of people who are not likely to divorce. (Read and remember the brief review which follows.)

2. That you can use this information to your advantage as you select your screening criteria.

Here is what the research says about the characteristics of people who are less likely to divorce:

1. Your level of education has a bearing on whether you are likely to divorce in the future. If you are a college-educated man or woman, your chance of marrying and divorcing is lower than for someone who has less education.[10]

2. Family background appears to make a difference. If you come from a family where your biological parents live in marriage and have not divorced, your chance of divorcing is lower than if you came from a broken home.[11] Why is this? Since your parents did not divorce, you grew up seeing them hold their marriage together and from that example, learned coping skills that you can carry into your own relationship. This means you are *less likely to see divorce as an answer* when your marriage is in trouble than others whose parents divorced when their marriage was in trouble. However, if you are one of the many people whose folks divorced, don't give up; you can still make a good marriage. (Read chapters six, seven, eight, and nine for more on this topic.)

3. If you did not co-habit with anyone before marrying, you are less likely to divorce.[12] Although this research suggests that you not co-habit prior to marriage, I realize that co-habitation is more widely practiced than it used to be. If you have been or are now co-habiting, I advise that you be sure that you are ready for marriage and be extra careful in selecting your acceptance and rejection criteria.

4. If you marry someone who is similar to you in values, background, life goals, and religious beliefs, your chance of divorcing is decreased.[13] This means that even if you are attracted to someone of a very different background, religion, goals, and values, your chances of staying married are better if you marry someone who is similar to you. The novelty of a very different person quickly wears off. Over many years of marriage you do not want to be in continuous conflict with a spouse who has very different ideas about the most important aspects of life.

5. Your age at marriage is important. People who marry in their twenties or older are less likely to divorce.[14] When people marry in their teens, the risk of divorce is two to three times higher than if they wait until their twenties or later.

Make this information work for you. Keep it in mind as you establish your screening criteria. If possible, develop yourself so you acquire the characteristics of people who are less likely to divorce.

I want to caution against over-interpreting these findings. For example, if your parents divorced and you did not go to college, that does not mean that you as an individual will be unsuccessful in marriage. People who never attended college can make successful, enduring marriages. Even individuals with difficult personal histories can improve their chances of a good marriage, and in chapter seven I share one man's story who did just that.

Important Personality Characteristics

In addition to the divorce research findings, you also need to understand the importance of personality characteristics. You need to select a person who has the characteristics to work through the difficult times that come in all marriages. The following characteristics are needed to make a long-term marriage work:

- The ability to be considerate and understanding of how you and other people feel

- The ability to react in support of how other people feel so that others feel supported

- Being comfortable with oneself and constructive with time spent alone

- Not needing the stimuli of parties, shopping, traveling, or attention to be happy

- The ability to treat people with respect publicly and privately

- The ability to accommodate change and make changes

These characteristics form the core of a well-adjusted person. If you can marry a person who has these characteristics, it is likely that you will have a happy marriage because you will have a spouse who can support you throughout life.

Other characteristics such as loyalty, a sense of humor, good looks and intelligence are great assets but by themselves are not enough to make a marriage work.

Do not marry anyone hoping that their personality traits will change in the future. Most people do not change, even if you lovingly try to facilitate the change for them. You need to choose someone based on what you see, with your eyes wide open.

Now let's get started. Let's select your screening criteria.

Selecting Your Screening Criteria: Defining the Kind of Person You Want to Marry

Keep your eyes wide open and follow these steps. Take these steps when you are not in love or distracted by a relationship.

1. Review your past relationships and identify what went wrong. What led to your poor choices? What decisions did you make wrongly? Looking back, what would you have done differently? (If you have not had a relationship yet, think of someone else's relationship you admire and ask the same questions.)

2. Think through the myths you may have held that led to poor relationships? Identify them. These beliefs are your weaknesses. Write them down. You want to remember what kind of mythical thinking you are prone to so you can avoid it in the future.

3. Think about the kind of a person you would be happy with in a long-term marriage. Use any words you like. Be very honest and specific. This is not a time to be politically correct.

4. Make a written listing of the characteristics you are looking for in a person. Having this list serves to remind you of what you want. Read your list over to make sure it says exactly what you mean to say. These are your acceptance screening criteria.

5. Decide what is unacceptable to you in another person. Be very honest with yourself. These are traits or personal histories that will disqualify a person from becoming your spouse and the parent of your children. Write these down as well. These are your rejection screening criteria.

6. Stick to what you decided. Changes to these lists should be made only after careful consideration. Your two lists will help you maintain a firm mental grasp on the kind of person you are looking for so you do not waste time pursuing unproductive relationships with unsuitable persons.

If you followed the steps you should have two lists. One is of the traits that you want to have in a person; the other is of the traits that you will not accept. Hold onto these; you will be using them later.

Characteristics of a Functional Marriage with a High Likelihood of Success

Consider the qualities needed for a well-functioning marriage by studying the circle diagram:

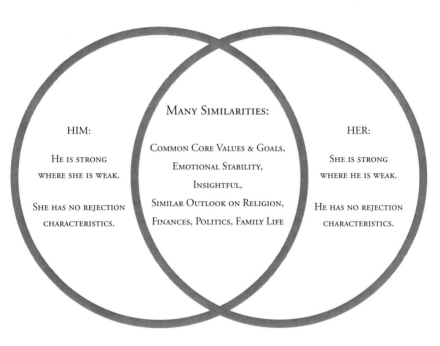

According to research, marriages have a higher likelihood of being successful if the persons have similar backgrounds, values, and ways of thinking.[15] These similarities are noted in the center, where the circles overlap each other. "Emotional stability" is a general phrase meaning that the persons are emotionally mature, have healthy personality characteristics, and take care of their mental health needs.

In the side parts of the circle, I noted two characteristics:

1. He and she accept each other's personal strengths and weaknesses. Based on this knowledge, they complement and willingly help each other. For example, she will take on family and household functions that he has no time or energy for, and he will voluntarily assume those functions that are difficult for her. She and he have the personality characteristics to work as a team and take care of all functions associated with their marriage.

2. He does not meet any of her rejection screening criteria. She does not meet any of his rejection screening criteria.

Marriages work well when couples complement each other and have no major differences. This is not to say that there are never any problems. Differences of opinion and occasional hurt feelings happen whenever people live together, but there will be fewer problems if the individuals have similar values, goals, religious orientation, political alliances, financial practices, and so forth.

Problems such as job loss, illness, and different parenting styles are better met if you and your spouse work together as a team. That way you bring both of your strengths to solving problems and coping with adversity. That is the way to build a deep, lasting marital bond.

Karen and Stu's Dysfunctional and Incompatible Marriage

Now compare the diagram of a successful marriage with one that was doomed to failure. The next circle diagram describes Karen and Stu's marriage, as discussed in chapter one.

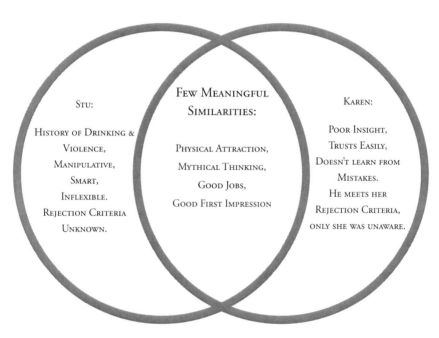

STU:

HISTORY OF DRINKING &
VIOLENCE,
MANIPULATIVE,
SMART,
INFLEXIBLE.
REJECTION CRITERIA
UNKNOWN.

FEW MEANINGFUL
SIMILARITIES:

PHYSICAL ATTRACTION,
MYTHICAL THINKING,
GOOD JOBS,
GOOD FIRST IMPRESSION

KAREN:

POOR INSIGHT,
TRUSTS EASILY,
DOESN'T LEARN FROM
MISTAKES.
HE MEETS HER
REJECTION CRITERIA,
ONLY SHE WAS UNAWARE.

The intersection of the two circles shows Karen and Stu's similarities. The remaining parts of the circles show Karen and Stu's individual traits and differences. Several things are noteworthy about this dysfunctional marriage:

First, Karen and Stu's similarities are based on superficial traits such as physical attraction and first impressions. These traits are unsuited to build the foundation of a stable, long-term marriage.

Second, Karen and Stu are very different people. Their individual personality traits make them incompatible. Their personal weaknesses make them a poor match for each other. Their marriage was destined for failure.

Third, this marriage could have been avoided if Karen had:

- Developed acceptance screening criteria that included "light social drinking only"

- Developed rejection screening criteria excluding a history of violence

- Protected herself by running a background check on Stu and found the DUI and violence on record prior to marrying him

- Given serious thought to why her first marriage ended in divorce, because then she would have waited longer to get to know Stu and most likely would not have married him

These actions might have prevented the immense pain of Karen's second divorce. You can avoid Karen's mistakes by keeping your eyes wide open and developing screening criteria for a good marriage. Your next step is to define each of your criteria as accurately as possible so they are worded exactly as you mean them. This means you need to form your ideas into concrete words. This is often difficult, as the following dialogues illustrate.

Helping Clients Select Acceptance Screening Criteria

Clients often use therapy to identify their screening criteria. I assist them in finding the words that best represent their ideas on what they want in a mate. The process goes something like this:

Me: "So what is important to you in a spouse?"

Client: "Well, Doc, my future wife has to be good looking."

Me: "I'm sorry, but I have no idea what you mean."

SUSANA K. O'HARA, PH.D.

Client: "You don't? You're the doc!"

Me: "I may be the doc, but I can't read your mind. I need you to be more specific. What does 'good looking' mean to you?"

Client: "Hmm…"

Me: "I am trying to figure out what you mean. Do you mean a Miss America good looking? Or a fit and healthy, sporty type? Or a clean, well-groomed woman who is a six or seven on a scale of ten? Or something else?"

Client: "I see. Well, let me think of what is really important to me."

We all tend to think and speak in generalities. The problem with this is that even unsuitable people will fit into loosely defined categories. That is why I encourage my clients to sharpen their thinking about acceptance criteria. When my client knows exactly what is important to him, he will not waste time with people who do not meet his criteria and, therefore, would be miserable being married to.

Client: "Here's what I mean. Good looking to me is a woman aged twenty-four to thirty, a six or seven on a scale of ten, with no tattoos or body piercings, who wears clean clothes and grooms herself well but is not heavy on makeup. That's better, isn't it?"

Me: "Yes. I understand much better what you mean. Anything else?"

Client (joking): "If she maintained a clean home, she would be even better looking to me! See how much I've thought this through, Doc?"

Next, the client and I discuss the woman's occupational status. Does he envision a working spouse or a stay-at-home, or a combination?

> Client: "Well, she has to have a job."

> Me: "What do you mean?"

> Client: "I have to get more specific, right?"

> Me: "Right. When you say your future wife has to have a job, that again is a very general statement. It could mean anything. Is a weekend babysitting job or bartending three nights a week okay with you? Or do you mean a job with regular hours and full benefits? What about income? How about job level? Is anything all right, or do you have a preference?"

> Client: "That is a lot to think about. I am not rich, so I guess it does matter. There's money and lifestyle and all that involved. I'll get back to you the next session."

The client eventually summarized a list of ten acceptance criteria. If he met a woman who met these criteria, he would be comfortable marrying her. His criteria are:

- A clean girl, six or seven on a scale of ten, preferably with no body art

- Someone who does not have to follow the latest trends in fashion or thinking

- Careful with money, has some savings, and little or no debt

- Same race as him

- Goes to work every day to a full-time job, but would be willing to be a stay-at-home mom

- Has at least a high-school education

- Believes in God and has a similar religious background

- Does not swear in public or private

- Realizes that a positive attitude is important and tries to maintain one

- Does not cheat or flirt and acts like a lady when socializing

I am including this person's criteria list as an example of how very specific I advise you to be in making up your criteria. This list and other lists contained in this book and its Appendix are simply examples of what other people felt was right for them. It is very important that you make up your own mind about what is important to you in choosing a marital partner.

For many people, stating these simple criteria is a difficult, self-discovery process. They start with vague feelings about what they want in a person. They wonder if they aren't taking the romance out of it by being objective. They wonder if they shouldn't just listen to their heart because it is hard to think. Then they struggle to create accurate verbal descriptions. Sometimes they struggle to not be afraid to say what they think; they do not want to be politically incorrect. I emphasize that the choice of a spouse is much too important to be influenced by the social/political trends of the day. People just need to say what kind of person they can be happy with.

Stating your criteria means you clearly understand what you want. It can change the way you used to think about people and the types of people you date.

3

⁓⁓⁓

Saying Hello and Getting the Most Out of What Happens

"Never let a fool kiss you and never let a kiss fool you."
Sign in an Irish Restaurant

With your criteria in mind, you are ready to evaluate people in a whole new way. You will scrutinize people with an eyes-wide-open strategy. Your overall goals are to talk to people with a clear purpose in mind, to not waste time talking about unimportant things, to make the most of time by talking about important things, and to figure out if a person meets your criteria or not.

If you ask focused questions and listen carefully, you should be able to figure out who is likely to be right for you.

At first it may seem unusual to structure conversations using criteria. However, you can get used to doing it. With practice, you can learn to ask questions and evaluate answers in a fluid, natural conversation.

The First Meeting

Before you meet someone, review what you want to find out. This is your conversation strategy. Your strategy should focus on:

- What you want to talk about (your criteria, to see if the person meets them or not)

- What you do not want to do (engage in too much small talk on frivolous topics, etc)

- How to guide the conversation the way you want it to go

- How to make the most of the face-to-face time you have

- How to determine if a person is receptive to you

- How to tell if the person responds to you appropriately

- How to exit a conversation when you want to

Your overall strategy is to talk to people in a purposeful way. This is because you want to find out what you want to know. No one else can do this for you.

People are usually most honest when you first meet them. This is because they do not know you well enough to know the answers you want to hear. That is why I suggest you ask your most important criteria-related questions in your first conversations.

Let's take a typical example of a first meeting. You are a woman who just met an interesting and reasonably attractive man. You decide to get to know him better, so you will start a "purposeful conversation." (Whenever I use this phrase, I am referring to conversations that relate to your criteria.)

Conversations can be started at any point; there is no perfect timing or questioning. Pick a topic to introduce the conversation. "Are you from around here?" "How did you hear about this event?" or similar open-ended questions are acceptable conversation starters.

Use open-ended questions whenever you want the other person to talk. How and what the person says in response to your question lets you gauge her or his responsiveness to you. One of two things usually happens. The first is that the person responds with an "I don't know" or some other simple words and/or does not look at you. From this you get the feeling that he or she does not want to talk to you. In this case, do not waste your time. Move on. Talk to someone else.

In the second case, the person looks you in the eye, gives you a courteous response, and asks you a question in turn. This type of a response is encouraging and serves as a possible signal that the person is interested in talking to you. In this case, you can test the waters by starting a purposeful conversation centered on your criteria.

Making Purposeful Conversation

Learning to question someone without being too obvious takes practice. However, you can learn to ask questions, anticipate the other person's answers, and keep conversations going. It is important to master these conversation skills if you want to find out if a person meets your criteria.

Susan decided to learn. Introverted by nature, Susan overcame her natural shyness and forced herself to talk to men. Samples of her purposeful conversations with men are reconstructed here as she described them to me. To follow Susan's conversations, you first need to know her acceptance and rejection screening criteria.

Susan's acceptance screening criteria are:

- Good family background

- He wants to marry and have a family

- Is able to socialize with a variety of people

- Is a high school, preferably college graduate

- Is honest

- Is reliable

- Has a similar or same religious faith

- Is a hard worker

- Is willing and able to do some household repairs

- Is reasonably good looking

Susan's rejection screening criteria are:

- A smoker, cigarettes or otherwise

- Any kind of drug abuse (legal or illegal)

- DUI or jail term history

- Unemployed or frequent job changes

- Debts over $5,000, not including a car payment or mortgage on a house

- Poor hygiene

- Poor vocabulary

- Swears or uses swear words in his speech

- Does not like to read

- Is unkind to his parents

What follows are examples of when Susan's conversations are going well or are not worth continuing.

Example of When Susan's Criteria-Related Conversation Is Going Right

"Hi, my name is Susan Black."

"Hello, I am Anthony Stone."

"Are you from around here, Anthony?"

"Yes, I grew up in the next town over, and I still have family living there. I myself live about fifty miles up the road. How about you, Susan?"

So far the conversation is going well. Anthony responded to Susan's interest in him and signaled his own interest back. Susan can now decide if she wants to continue the conversation. A natural extension of the conversation might happen in the following way:

"I grew up a few towns over too. But my job is in the city now. Which town did you grow up in, Anthony?"

"Johnsonville. My family lived on Maple Avenue. Actually my brother still lives in the family home. And yourself?"

"I grew up in Bristol, and we played the Johnsonville softball team each spring. Against your high school, we came out on the losing end most of the time."

"So you were on the softball team? I was on the football team. One of my teammates was dating a girl on your softball team, I think. Let me see if I remember her name. It was Cynthia Albright, and she played third base. Is that right?"

So far, so good. At this point Susan has to decide what to talk about next. She knows that she and Anthony are talking well; Anthony is able to absorb and reciprocate her conversation. Also, Anthony has shared enough information about himself so that Susan could inquire about the family and do background checks if necessary. Susan appreciates the fact that Anthony is voluntarily sharing this information. Maybe he is inviting her to find out more about him. So she decides to steer the conversation in the direction of her acceptance criteria (good family background). She will talk about her own family and then ask Anthony about his.

"Yes, I remember Cynthia. She was a senior on the team when I joined as a freshman. My family came to my games, and they would remark on what a fine ballplayer she was. It was helpful to me to have my family there because we could talk about things afterward like which players did well or made errors. It helped me to learn the game."

Susan then asks Anthony, "How much was your family involved in your football?"

His response is immediate. "Quite a bit. It was a social outing for my parents and grandparents. My father made it a point to come to two of my practices each week, besides the games. He just enjoyed seeing what the team was doing, and we would talk about it later."

"Oh, that sounds like my folks. What are your parents like as people?"

Since the conversation is going well, Susan decides to steer it deeper as she asks Anthony to describe his parents. She was careful to use an open-ended question such as "What are they like as people?" This is important, because now Anthony has to decide how to talk, what to say, and which family members to talk about. This takes mental effort, and Susan will see just how Anthony responds. From that she will have a sense for the sophistication of his thinking and what he is like as a person.

Whenever you ask people about their parents, you will get a lot of information about the people themselves. In this case, whatever Anthony says about his parents will reveal his attitude toward them. Susan is waiting to hear what he says and how he will say it.

Anthony's tone is relaxed as he responds, "Oh, I'd say they are regular people. My parents are both retired. I go visit every other weekend, and we talk on the phone every few days. They were always there for my brother and me, so I try to be there for them. Know what I mean?"

This brief speech counts as a quality response. First, Anthony shows Susan respect by giving her a direct response. Second, he gives an appropriate general response about his parents, as though he has thought through the pluses and minuses of his upbringing. His use of the adjective "regular" can mean that his parents may have their good and bad points, but Anthony values them as people and has a sense of loyalty to them. Most importantly, Anthony emphasizes that he values reciprocating for what his parents have done for him. His speech appears to indicate that Anthony understands the value of family and how a family works.

The purposeful conversation is off to a good start. Susan may continue to raise other topics on her criteria list. If she does, she will find out more about Anthony and whether he meets her acceptance and rejection criteria.

Example of When Susan's Criteria-related Conversation Is Not Worth Continuing

"Hi, my name is Susan Black."

"I'm Danny."

"Are you from around here?"

"Not exactly."

"Where are you from?"

"What is this, Susan, Twenty Questions?"

Time to exit the conversation. Danny is too much of a problem. He does not get it that he should be respectful. First, he did not give his last name, as would be expected by courtesy, since Susan gave her last name. Second, he adopted a defensive posture to a very routine question. His defensiveness led him to an offensive posture: "What is this, Twenty Questions?" and to imply that Susan is out of line asking him where he is from.

If Susan were Danny's therapist, she might want to know the source of his defensiveness. However, Susan is looking for someone to marry, not to nurture some mixed-up man. Susan does not need to find out why Danny is being rude to her, because she already knows that she is wasting her time talking to him.

Danny looks at Susan as though she has wronged him by asking him where he is from. He expects an apology. Well, Susan owes Danny nothing. What Susan needs to do is to gracefully exit the conversation. She is not going to let Danny know what she is thinking because she's not investing any more energy into talking with him.

"My mistake, Danny," Susan says, reaching for her cell phone. "Excuse me, my sister (mother, office, girlfriend, Realtor, boss) is calling. It's important," and she moves away from him.

Here is another example of a conversation not worth continuing. (This man is from the same high school as Anthony Stone, but the similarity ends there.)

"Hi, my name is Susan Black."

"Hello, I am Jonathan Smith."

"Are you from around here, Jonathan?"

"Yes, I grew up in the next town over, but I myself live about fifty miles up the road. And you?"

"I grew up a few towns over too. But my job is in the city now. Which town around here did you grow up in, Jonathan?"

"In a crappy little place called Johnsonville. Glad to be out of there. Rarely go back there if I can help it. Well, maybe for the holidays, if Ma really wants me to."

A pause ensues. Jonathan thinks that Susan is worth talking to so he says, "Where are you from?"

"I grew up in Bristol. Hey, I played against the Johnsonville softball team each spring. I am sorry to say that we came out on the losing end."

"Well, I never cared for the high school teams much. I spent as little time in school as I could. Guess I barely graduated. But you could not tell that from where I am today. No, sir. I'm doing great!"

Since high school grades are the best predictors of college success, and since Jonathan barely graduated from high school, Susan can assume that he did not graduate from college. That in itself is not a problem; some successful people never graduate from college. But why, if he is successful now, is Jonathan still negative about his high school?

What is most troubling in Jonathan's response is that he does not appear to have come to terms emotionally with his past. His insecurity propels him to advertise how well he is doing now, even though Susan did not ask him about that. Emphasizing his current success may be his way of reassuring himself, trying to impress Susan, or both. Either way, it is sad. Nonetheless, Susan decides to continue talking to him, if only to practice asking about her criteria. She makes up her mind to ask him about his feelings for his family.

"I am glad that you are doing well, Jonathan. You were mentioning that you might go home for the holidays, if your ma wanted you to. What have you got for family, Jonathan? What are your folks like?"

"Oh my God, every woman wants to talk about family," Jonathan says, displaying his insecurity again. "I don't get it, never have. But since you brought it up, I'll tell you. My parents are a mess, always have been. Ma, I can take once a year. I'll see her then. And families are nuts. I see no sense in getting married, you know what I mean? If you are in love, you don't need a piece of paper from the government to say you are married. I know I don't want kids. Kids just get in the way of things. I've got my sights set high, and I am going to do other stuff."

By this time Susan has had it. "That is great, Jonathan, and I really wish you well," she says, checking her cell messages. "Gosh, here's a message from my mom (sister, neighbor, accountant, office, etc). I want to call her right back. Would you please excuse me?"

Susan moves away to make the call. She has no intention of resuming her conversation with Jonathan. In a few minutes she found out everything she needed to know. Jonathan does not meet one of her most important acceptance criteria (which is to marry and have a family). When she finishes her make-believe phone call, she will look for someone else to talk to.

By asking her criteria questions clearly and openly, Susan realized that Jonathan did not have the type of family background she was looking for. He also did not have any desire to marry or to have a family of his own. His reasons for not having a family may be perfectly justified; Susan does not have to know his reasons. Jonathan's choice to do other things with his life may be the best decision for him. Susan was wise to politely end the conversation.

I want to note that many people had a turbulent or sad childhood. While none of us has control over who we are born to, we do have some control over what we do with our own lives. Children of alcoholic or mentally ill parents and children who have been abandoned often have difficulty talking about their families in a constructive manner. However, many are able to move on. People who manage their own lives well are generally less critical of their parents. They are not likely to badmouth their family members publicly, especially to someone they just met.

As people mature, they realize that no family or person is perfect. This realization helps to soften past family issues and lets the person move on to making a better present and future for themselves. It is a way of making up for the past. If a person has done this and someone asks about his parents, the person will answer in general, respectful, and reserved terms. The absence of this respectful quality makes Jonathan's response especially troubling. He seems immature.

For example, if Jonathan was at peace with his past, he might give a more mature response such as:

"Susan, you asked about my high school years. I did a lot of growing up then. I should have made more out of those years, but I didn't. However, I am now making up for lost time. I think I am doing pretty well and have laid out a path for my future."

About his parents, a more emotionally mature Jonathan might have said the following:

"Susan, my folks had problems, and they couldn't raise me the way other kids were raised. But they did the best they could with what they had. If I ever have a family of my own, I would need to be married to someone who had a strong family background and a good idea on how to raise children."

There are two major reasons for asking people criteria-related questions. One is to see if they match your criteria. The other is to see how they respond to the questions themselves. You have to learn to listen for the quality and maturity of a response. Does the person give a mature, well-thought-out response to your question? If so, it may indicate emotional depth and an ability to evaluate himself and his life. Or does the person become defensive or agitated when he has to respond to a question he doesn't want to hear? If you listen carefully, you will be able to tell which it is.

The type of response you get indicates how this person will handle life's difficulties, should the two of you ever marry.

Using Complex, Open-Ended Questions

Complex, open-ended questions can be asked if you notice contradictions between behavior and speech. For example, if a person says one thing and does something contrary to what she said, it is important to ask for an explanation. Maybe it is you who misunderstood something, but it is also possible that the person is being inconsistent; i.e. they talk the talk, but they don't walk the walk. Examples of complex, open-ended questions are:

- "I recall your saying that you do not want to have children. But when you are around your nephews and nieces, you seem to like them, and they really like you. How is that?"

- "I get that you are very interested in being with me because you said so. Then when we get together, I usually need to do what you planned and what you like to do and work around your schedule. So I hear the words, but I do not see the actions supporting the words. How is that?"

My clients sometimes hesitate to ask such questions, saying, "Whoa! I don't think I could ever be so confrontational!"

Well, it is never too late to learn. If you are serious about getting to know someone, sometimes this is what you need to do. Especially if you are looking for someone to marry, you have every right to ask questions. If the other person is right for you, you will get satisfactory answers and you will be pleased.

Needless to say, you need to ask the questions in a nice way. Also, it is important to remember that everyone is inconsistent sometimes. Mature people readily admit to their occasional inconsistencies, while immature people tend to become defensive. So when you confront, watch for the following:

- How did this person respond to a gentle confrontation?

- Did the person understand what I was asking?

- Did the person appreciate my honesty in asking the question?

- Is the person willing to concede that I may have a point?

- Can they see humor in their own imperfection?

- Did I get a coherent answer to my question?

The kind of response you get tells you a great deal about the person.

Examples of Poor-quality Responses

"Hey, babe, when I tell you I am interested in you, just take it. Okay? You have no idea how much effort I put into showing you a good time."

"You need to relax. Okay? Just enjoy the places I take you to. Don't ask questions."

"Well, it's like this. I'm not your typical woman, see? Having my own kids and playing with my nephews are two different things. I don't know why. I don't think about it, so don't try to make me."

Inflexibility is the common element in all three responses. It means that the person is not likely to change. Not only that, they won't even give a courteous answer. They do not want to think about what you say, so they penalize you for thinking and for asking a reasonable question. A person who responds like this prior to marriage will be just like this or worse once married.

My suggestion? If you hear something like this, move on. Do it quickly. You are not likely to have a purposeful conversation with this type of person. You wouldn't have a good time being married to one either.

Using Closed Questions on Purpose

When you want a very direct answer (a yes or no) to a question, use what we call closed questions. Honest people will give a direct answer. People who are uncomfortable give evasive answers. As you search for someone to marry, you want to find out what kind of a person you are talking to as soon as possible.

Example A. Susan continues talking to Anthony. She decides to ask a question about how frequently he has been unemployed (one of her rejection criteria). Susan steers the conversation toward work in order to set up a closed question for Anthony to answer.

"I work in the city," Susan says, continuing their conversation, "but I want to change my job. To do that, I may have to be out of work for a while."

Then she asks the closed question she really wants to know the answer to: "Have you ever been out of work for a while, Anthony?"

This question requires a yes or no answer, and Anthony has to make a choice. If he doesn't care about Susan, or if he has been out of work a lot and wants to hide that fact, he can evade this direct question. An evasive answer is something like:

"Oh, let me try to remember. I don't think so. Well, maybe once or twice. I was in between jobs here and there."

This answer is evasive and suspect because people remember being unemployed. The anxiety associated with little or no money coming in and bills waiting to be paid is not forgotten, unless the person is a slacker and a freeloader to begin with.

An honest, direct answer is, "Yes, five years ago. There was a layoff, and it took me six months to find another job."

Susan's well-placed, closed question and Anthony's response will satisfy Susan's need to know whether he meets her criteria.

Example B. In this case, Susan wants to see if Anthony meets her rejection criteria concerning drug use. From therapy, Susan knows that a good time to ask about substance abuse is when you first meet someone, *before* the other person knows you well enough to know what answer you want to hear.

The two of them are in a room full of people. With her drug use criterion in mind, Susan says to Anthony, "I see some people leaving. I think they are going to have a smoke. Do you want to go?"

"No. I don't smoke. I don't want to mess up my lungs."

"Do any drugs?"

"Oh, I like a good buzz every now and then. And I do speed sometimes."

Susan found out what she wanted to know. She may need to ask more questions to decide if the good buzz and using speed amounts to drug abuse. Although Anthony seems honest enough, there are many people (like Stu in chapter one) who are on good behavior and minimize their drug use activities until after they are married. So even though I encourage my clients to ask direct questions, I also advise them to do thorough background checks (see chapter five) to verify information they receive.

Susan did a great job asking her questions. Her closed, direct questions got her direct answers. She can now better figure out if Anthony meets her criteria for marriage.

Your Time Is Precious: Keep Small Talk to a Minimum

Our lives are full of small talk. We use it to put each other at ease. Casual conversations about weather, sports, crafts, cars, or clothes are relatively safe topics designed to avoid arguments and let people relax with each other.

Because small talk allows us to socialize in a relaxed manner, we tend to do a lot of it when we first meet people. However, when you want to get to know someone pretty quickly, small talk can be a waste of time.

Your time is precious because you want to figure out if the person meets your acceptance and rejection criteria *before* you fall in love. Should you fall in love prior, you tend to disregard your screening criteria. When a person is in love, objective thinking is often suspended. The hijacked brain automatically starts excusing even the biggest of faults of the beloved person. Acceptance and rejection screening criteria are simply ignored.

Your time is also precious because you don't want to waste any of it. If one person does not meet your criteria, you want to move right along to meeting others. You do not want to spend months or years dating someone you will never marry.

"Big talk," on the other hand, is talk about money, politics, religion, personal relationships, and other deep issues. Big talk is when you really find out what a person is like. Talking about your criteria is big talk. You are conducting the interviews of your lifetime.

Listening for Style vs. Substance

Big talk is talking about the substance of a person. It is the substance of the other person (as well as your own) that will make or break the marriage. The most attractive and stylistic people become boring and annoying if they have little or no substance, and you are stuck with him or her for a lifetime.

The style of the person is the part you notice first. For example, you can see if a person is introverted, extroverted, easy or hard to talk to, flamboyant, or reserved. You can also see style in the objects, clothes, and toys he or she has. Everyone has a distinctive style. Some people do not care what they look like; that is their style.

Substance is the depth of people's thinking and feeling. This includes their morals, character, the ideas they hold dear, their emotional makeup, personality traits, and code of conduct. Substance determines whether a person chooses the right or wrong thing to do when no one is looking.

When I teach this concept in therapy, I ask clients to imagine a room full of books on bookcases. The books sitting on the shelves are like people. They are waiting to be read. The saying "you can't tell a book by its cover" applies to people as well. With books and people, what do you see first? The physical appearance, the style of the cover. Some people look great and have great style. They have a gift for putting you at ease. Other people are so-so; they are books with unattractive covers.

At a typical social gathering of people, what you really see is a lot of book covers. People exhibit their personalities like books exhibit their covers. Some people look really good, have great small talk conversation, and sparkle in public. Initially, it is easy to be attracted to them. Guard yourself against falling in love with a person's cover, because then you are in love with the style of the person without knowing the substance.

In both books and people, there are four general combinations of substance and style:

1. A great style and no substance. This person is like a book with a very attractive cover but nothing worth reading. Books like this are similar to people who have nothing interesting or useful to say; the person is physically attractive, but not much more. It is not until you open the covers and read the book to its end that you realize there is no substance or that you do not like what the book says. Similarly, you have to get to know a person before you decide if you like or dislike their substance. Some of the most stylistically attractive people have little or no substance to them.

2. A great style and great substance. A person with a great style can also have good substance. Again, you have to get by the cover first to read the whole book and get to know the person inside.

3. No style and no substance. There are people who have little or no style and also no substance. These people have boring covers and have little interesting to say.

4. No style and great substance. These are the books with boring covers but lots of good reading inside. These are books that you can keep reading over and over, and each time you find something new to think about. In many cases, people with no style are very interesting to talk to, so their lack of style is not seen as a deficit. Their substance is so attractive that you might want to spend your whole life talking with them. People with no style take a little extra effort to get to know. However, once they get going, these people readily and happily engage in purposeful conversations.

Practice Conversations with LIFE Topics

Do you have trouble talking to strangers? Do you get anxious when it is time to talk about your criteria? If so, your conversations may flow better using the mnemonic device of LIFE. LIFE makes it easier to think of conversation topics. It should be easy to remember the word LIFE because it is your life that you are trying to improve by marrying well.

In LIFE, each letter stands for something that you can ask another person a question about:

L is for livelihood; how a person makes a living.

I is for inspiration, the kinds of things that motivate a person.

F is for family and friends.

E is for entertainment, such as what a person likes to do in his or her spare time.

The more people you talk to, the more practiced you become. You will meet people with distinct and interesting personalities. You will become better and better at sizing up your fellow human beings. Eventually you will relax and enjoy yourself.

Lastly, remember the following:

- Do not worry about whether people like you. Not everyone will—accept it. This is not a popularity contest. This is all about looking for one person to have a lifelong marriage with. You probably will meet many people before you find someone who meets your criteria.

- What is most important is how well you like the people you meet. The goal is a no-divorce marriage, and it does require due diligence on your part.

- These are the interviews of your lifetime. Relax and make the most of them.

As you go about meeting people, guard your physical and emotional safety. In the next chapter I cite some commonsense safeguards, which come from the experiences of many people. Although they are not foolproof, people have found them to be of considerable assistance. I hope you will as well.

4

～～

USING COMMON SENSE TO PROTECT YOURSELF

"Better safe than sorry."

American Idiom

Meeting people is more enjoyable when you feel safe and secure in your surroundings. The purpose of this chapter is to emphasize the safety features most important to your security. Both men and women need to protect their physical and emotional safety.

Do not hesitate to employ these safeguards even if people tease you about it. You are simply being prudent in your actions and thinking. You are not being paranoid if you use common sense to protect yourself.

Know the Difference Between Prudence and Paranoia

It is important that you understand the difference between prudence and paranoia because it is a great difference.

Prudence is defined as using good judgment. It also means having careful forethought and a regard for one's own interests.

For example, you show good judgment if you decide to conduct an online search of public domain information about someone you just met. Other times it will be reasonable for you to do a more thorough screening. You show careful forethought if you employ the safeguards you read about here. You must act in your own interest, because no one else can do it for you.

Paranoia is very different from prudence. Because many lay-people misuse the word *paranoia*, I am including Webster's definition of it: "Paranoia is a serious mental condition. Paranoia is disturbed thinking which causes a person to be extremely anxious or fearful, often to the point of irrationality or delusions."

The safety precautions suggested in this chapter have nothing to do with being clinically paranoid. If someone should tease you (or become confrontational) about your insistence on safety, just say, "No. I'm not at all paranoid. But I am being prudent."

Then smile. If the person does not know what paranoia is, he probably does not know what prudent means either.

Being Prudent When Meeting People

The following suggestions are the collective wisdom of people who came before you and learned to protect themselves the hard way. It does not include every safeguard, just some of the major ones. It is prudent to consider all of these suggestions when meeting people for the first or second time.

Keep the focus on your goal. Your goal is to get to know people, gather information, and decide whether they meet your screening criteria. Therefore, your thoughts and movements need to be connected to your goal.

Go to familiar places to socialize. Consider this a home field advantage. People are most comfortable in those parts of town and establishments they know well. When you select your home turf for a meeting with someone, you will probably be more relaxed and show yourself that way. That is because you have avoided the stress of going to an unfamiliar place, neighborhood, bus stop, subway, or parking garage. If you are relaxed, you can better focus on your goal. Another advantage of meeting in a place familiar to you is that local people know who you are, if only by sight.

Meet in public places with other people around. This is for your protection whether you are a man or a woman. Do not make exceptions to this rule.

Make short, simple dates at first. An attractive, recently divorced lady said, "I have already learned to meet people over lattes rather than dinner."

"How do you mean?"

"Well, once or twice I agreed to have dinner with people I had never met before. Ten minutes into the appetizers I saw that we were not a good match. Let me tell you, the rest of the dinner was a waste of time and money.

"From then on, I promised myself that I would never struggle through dinner again. My current policy is to meet new people for coffee at the corner store. That way we can sip coffee for half an hour to two hours, depending on how much time I want to spend."

Know the address and phone number. Wherever you go, get this information. Also, have a taxi's number on speed dial in your cell phone. This will let you quickly exit any uncomfortable situations. In case you are lost, parked somewhere strange, or afraid of going into a parking lot by yourself, call 911. You will be routed to the police, and they will come to the address you give them. They will help you out.

Have a plan. The plan should include when you arrive at a place, how long you will stay, and when you expect to return home. These are estimated time intervals. Inform your friends, roommates, or parents of your plan. Stick to your plan. Once you are out, do not change plans or accept unexpected invitations to another location, unless you are familiar with the new place and comfortable going.

Take along a wingman. *Wingman* is a military term for someone who watches your back and protects your interests. If you travel out of your neighborhood or city, take a trusted friend with you. For example, if you are invited to a social event at a strange college campus, request that a friend be able to come along. It is best if you and your friend can attend events together. If that is not possible, your friend should stay nearby. I recommend this safety feature for both males and females.

Observe the reaction of the person who invited you when you ask to bring a friend along. Their reaction may surprise you. If the person does not like your bringing someone along, ask why. What sort of entertainment was being planned that a friend of yours could not join?

If you cannot take a friend, make sure a trusted person knows exactly where you are going to be. Call this person every few hours to confirm where you are and when you are safe at home. Have them call you while you are out.

Trust your instincts. Sometimes it is your body that tells you that you are uncomfortable, especially if your brain has no concrete information of danger to yourself. There are several bodily sensations that clients and others have felt when they are feeling uncomfortable with their environment. Some of these body sensations are:

- any part of your body tensing up

- your stomach churning,

- a headache developing

- feelings of sudden tiredness

- heart beating faster

- hands getting cold or sweaty

- feelings of general anxiety

- feelings of wanting to get out of wherever you are

These sensations caution you against continuing what you are doing. They are telling you to get out of the situation. You do not have to understand why. You do not have to explain anything to anyone. Get yourself out of the situation and somewhere safe. Sort it out later.

Never go into a neighborhood or enter an establishment that you do not like the looks of. If your instincts signal that something is not right, get out of there. Your safety and comfort are much more important than keeping an appointment.

Be prepared for the unexpected. Have an exit strategy. Men and women are equally at risk in unfamiliar situations and can be targeted in various ways. Both men and women should be wary of a stranger taking a quick interest in them. If your instincts signal that something is wrong, listen and act on them. Use your preplanned exit strategy. This may be as simple as calling a taxi (from the speed dial on your cell phone) or a friend to come get you. Again, you do not need to make excuses. You can sort it out later.

Abstain or keep alcohol to a minimum. Remember your goal. Your goal is to safely meet and evaluate people to see if they meet your screening criteria. You are not out to drink. You do not care if anyone wants you to drink.

If you have an alcohol problem, get help for it before dating and marrying. If you are a recovering alcoholic, socialize at establishments where no alcohol is served.

Be careful with the drinks you are offered. When at a party or gathering, open up your own can of beverage. Do not drink out of anything that is passed around. If you wish, you can take your own favorite drink along and cite a special dietary need as your reason for doing so. ("I don't want the calories," or "I'm on a training diet" are common reasons.) In a restaurant, only accept drinks from the waiter's or bartender's own hands. If you leave your table to go to the bathroom or to make a call, consider ordering a fresh beverage upon your return if you are uncomfortable.

Do not stay out if you do not feel well. If you get sick while you are out, do not accept a ride from a new date. Call a taxi (speed dial) to take you home or an ambulance (911) to take you to the hospital.

Always make sure your cell phone is fully charged before going out.

Carry pepper spray in your pocket or pocketbook. Most people never use their sprays but feel the comfort of having it for protection. Practice using the spray (aim at a post or bush) so that you are practiced in its use and know what to expect when you have to use it. Most sprays reach a distance of about ten feet.

In many states you need a license to carry pepper spray. This license can be obtained from your local police department. Usually it is an easy process. Always have this license with you.

You cannot carry the spray when flying on commercial airlines or entering a building where your belongings are screened (such as a courthouse). Should your pepper spray be found during a search and you do not have the license to carry on your person, the authorities will have to detain you.

Finally, if you have to use the spray, do so. Just the act of your drawing the spray may prevent further confrontation. (Predators don't like confrontations; they like easy prey.) If that does not work, use the spray. If it turns out that you made a mistake, apologize and state that you used it because you were afraid.

Dress and behave modestly. If you are rich or well to do, do not advertise it. The very appearance of being well off makes you a target. Do not wear your best jewelry or drive your best car when you go to meet new people. You do not want a person to like you for your wealth. You want him or her to like you for yourself.

Do not dress in a sexually provocative manner. You want someone who loves you for yourself, not for your looks. Dress modestly. Present yourself so the other person can get to know the real you.

Be safe on the Internet. Protect your personal information. Realize that once you release personal information on the Internet, it is no longer in your control and could fall into the wrong hands.

If you want to be respected, act accordingly. Make sure your e-mail account has a respectable address, something your grandmother would not blush to see. Racy e-mail addresses invite attention from the wrong kind of people. Also, your e-mail address should not contain your real name.

Information you should always protect are: your name, where you live, social security number, where you work, specifics about your income and assets, your telephone number, and information about your family and family assets. You can add to this list, but do not subtract from it.

You should have an unlisted landline telephone number. The reason for this is that the Internet has a feature called the "reverse white pages lookup." Using this feature, someone can find your name and home address, thereby revealing the information you want to protect.

If you have an unlisted number, your home address is not listed or accessible. If your home address is unknown, you are less likely to be stalked or have someone show up at your door begging you to see them.

Be careful transitioning from a Web site to private e-mailing as you develop communication with a new person. Only after extensive private e-mailing would you exchange first names and, if things progress well, cell phone numbers.

Realize that predators like easy prey. If you follow these safety rules, nasty people with bad intentions are more likely to leave you alone. For example, if on an evening out you are observed to be abstaining from alcohol and drugs and calling to check in with your friends, mom, or dad, anyone intending to harm you will realize that you have a strong safety network of people and rules that you follow. This protection makes you undesirable as a target. Both male and female predators want to get away with their abuse, so they will seek out someone who is under the influence and not well protected.

Lastly, check out information you get. People may say things to impress you. Others may say things to mislead you. How can you tell if someone's lying? In the next chapter I discuss how to detect lying. I also explain how you can check out whether the information you are given is true or not.

5

How to Tell If Someone Is Lying and What to Do about It

Exercise due diligence in case your date
is not exercising due disclosure.

Thomas P. O'Hara

How can you detect liars and protect yourself against their lies? There are ways to do this. I will start by describing the research on lying and the most common ways that people lie.

Although most children are taught to not lie, lying is fairly common. There is much research about lies and how to detect a liar. Googling the topic is worthwhile. Research shows that most people are poor lie detectors.[16] Even specially trained people such as CIA agents, experienced detectives, and Secret Service Personnel only achieve about 70 percent accuracy-detecting lies.[17] The average person does much worse.

My formal training as a lie detector started in graduate school when I was assigned my first real client. Until that time I assumed that people did not lie. I mean, why would someone lie, especially in therapy? Doesn't everyone speak the truth to their therapist? I was young and naïve.

It is a good thing my professors listened to tapes of all my conversations with clients (for three years in a row, actually). Based on their feedback, I realized I did not know how to listen. Then I learned to listen to what people said and did not say. I learned that people lie and that they do it in different ways.

Trained observers can often detect nonverbal cues of lying by carefully watching a person's body language and facial expressions. However, it is easier to lie with words because words can be rehearsed ahead of time.[18] Many liars carefully rehearse their lies by selecting the words that best accomplish the deceit. For this reason, this chapter focuses on how people use words to lie.

Some years ago I started keeping a list of the common ways that people lie. I did this for the education and protection of my clients. The following is my categorization of the most frequent ways people lie, distort, and misrepresent the truth.

The "You are Meeting Me at My Best" Lie

It is natural for people to want to make a good first impression. They dress and groom themselves, shake hands, smile, and talk appropriately. Single people hoping to get married especially want to make a good first impression.

Sometimes the good impression is so overdone that a false presentation is created. This false presentation amounts to a lie.

For example, my client Susie gets ready for a party where she knows she will be introduced to Jim. Susie knows how to look good and how to present herself as interesting. She is spunky because she has just taken a little (over the counter) "alert" pill. She also spent money on tanning, nails, perfume, and clothes to look pretty. Her mood is vibrant, hypomanic. When Jim meets Susie, he sees an attractive, sparkling conversationalist.

Jim then thinks, *Wow! This may be the woman I have been waiting to meet.*

But Jim is looking at a lie. Susie's presentation is a lie because normally she is a depressed and unorganized person. The truth is that her finances are a mess. She should not have spent money on tanning, nails, perfume, and clothes, because she can't afford them. Susie has missed rent payments and is being evicted from her apartment. Nonetheless, she spent the money to keep her depression at bay for a few days and to impress Jim.

Why would Susie want to impress Jim? It is because she has figured out even before tonight's party that someone like Jim could be the answer to her problems. A nice man with a steady income is just what she really needed. Maybe, if she positioned things just right, Jim might find her attractive and help out.

Jim's job is to remember that you can't tell a book by its cover and that the style and the substance of a person can be very different. (See the chapter entitled "Saying Hello and Getting the Most Out of What Happens Next" for further discussion.) Jim's job is to get to know Susie better. He has to check out the information she gives him. Jim has to look beyond Susie's style and find out what her substance is. Furthermore, Jim has to be careful to not fall in love. He needs to talk about his criteria. He needs to take his time and check out information Susie gives him. He needs to do a background check.

If Jim is not careful, it will take him months to figure out that Susie is not as she presents herself. The truth is that she is just the opposite of how she presents; she has been lying to him.

Beware of appearances, especially if the appearance is very good. People tend to compensate for their shortcomings. Things may not be as they look and the person not as they advertise themselves.

The White Lie

The term *white* in white lie means that the lie itself is a harmless lie. Also known as a little white lie, it tends to be about relatively unimportant matters. This kind of lie is told to spare the feelings of another person. The following examples show what I mean.

Example A. Tom has not seen his grandmother for several months. Tom's family told Tom that Grandma has been sickly, and everyone in the family is trying to keep her spirits up. When Tom next sees his Grandma, he thinks to himself, *Poor Grandma, she looks awful.* But what he says to Grandma is, "Grandma, you look great!"

In reality, Grandma does look awful. But Tom says the white lie because he is fond of his grandma and wants to cheer her up.

Example B. Sharon is trying to select the right outfit to wear to a party. Because she does not trust her own judgment, she regularly consults Bob before making a wardrobe decision. Sharon says, probably for the thousandth time since they got married, "Honey, do you like this outfit? I am thinking of wearing it to the party tonight."

In truth, Bob hates the outfit. However, somewhere during the course of their marriage Bob decided that he would always make positive comments about Sharon's outfits because clothes are not worth fighting over. Bob saves his confrontations with Sharon for more important matters, such as when she runs up the credit card bill or fights with his mother. So in the matter of Sharon's outfit, he produces a little white lie: "Yes, hon, I like the outfit fine," and he is careful to smile and look at the outfit in question while he is lying. That way, Bob learned, Sharon is more likely to believe him.

When a person is caught in a white lie, an honest explanation for the lie should be produced. An apology is also in order because, even though the lie was little, it was still a lie.

A person who tells many repeated white lies and does not apologize for them when confronted may have an established pattern of lying. Read on for the description of a pathological liar.

The "Misdirection Lie," Also Known as the "Red Herring"

This is a simple one and easy to recognize once you understand the pattern.

It starts by someone asking a question. There is a problem, though. The person who should be providing the answer does not want to give it. The person will not say the truth because, if they did, it would make them look bad somehow. So what happens is that the person sidesteps the question and produces a diversion at the same time.

The following conversation between Bill and Sara shows how this is done. The couple has been dating for a year. Each maintains their own apartment. They occasionally talk about marriage. Both contribute to a joint savings account.

Bill thinks it would be nice if they could take some day trips together. So he says, "Hon, how much money is in the savings account? Can we use some of the money for day trips this summer?"

A simple question, you might say, but in Bill's relationship it is not. Instead of answering Bill, Sara becomes agitated.

"Now why did you have to bring that up? I have had such a terrible time with that account. I want you to tell everyone that our bank is awful. Do you know that when I went to check the balance, their computer system was down? I mean, down? Where else does that ever happen? I was so distraught!" Sara's face is contorted, and she is shaking her hands in the air.

Bill is alarmed that he caused Sara to get upset and rushes to console her. "Oh, honey, don't get upset. What can we do?"

"Do? I am going to refill my Lorazepam prescription, of course. This has got me so upset! I can't sleep at night. I work so darn hard to keep costs down. But everything is getting so much more expensive. I can't stand it. I am going to call my doctor's office right this minute and tell them to phone my pharmacy to refill my Lorazepam prescription. Oh, I just hate our bank!"

"Now, now," Bill says, trying to calm Sara. "Honey, calm yourself. Just take care of yourself and try to not worry."

Okay. What just happened in this conversation? Does something seem wrong? Yes, and it is called a red herring.

The simple sequence is that Bill asked Sara a legitimate question about their savings account. There should have been a simple answer, but Sara evaded the question because she did not want to say the truth. Even if the bank's system was down for a moment, Sara could have retrieved the balance later. But that is not what happened.

Instead of giving the proper answer, Sara displayed a series of evasive maneuvers. First, she badmouthed the bank and implied that she is conscientious about money. She then implied that the bank made her anxious, which caused her to lose sleep so that she'd have to call her doctor's office for anti-anxiety medication. Bill, thrown off guard by such an agitated response to a simple question, backed down from getting an answer.

If Bill takes the time to think about this verbal exchange, he should realize that because he was distracted by Sara's drama, he dared not pursue his question further. Bill should also get the feeling that something is not right with the savings account. If he is a passive person, he will not ask the question again. He will keep quiet and accept that he can't have the trip he was hoping for.

If he is a smart person, Bill will check the balance of the account himself and discuss with Sara whatever irregularities he finds. Bill should also remember that Sara said she would have to refill her anti-anxiety prescription. Refilling the prescription means that she used it before, so she may have an anxiety issue completely independent of the bank's actions and their savings. Did Bill know this beforehand? This is important because Sara's anxiety issue, drama, and avoidance of truthfully answering questions does have significance for Bill's relationship with her.

At the very least, Bill would be wise to rethink whether Sara should be handling their joint account. Overall, Bill needs to decide if Sara has a pattern of evading his questions. If he decides that she does, Bill should question if he wants to live his life with her.

Is Sara really the woman he should marry?

Psychologists refer to Sara's response as a red herring. A herring is a fish; when it starts to rot it turns smelly and red. It is so smelly that it attracts everybody's attention, thereby distracting a person from his or her original thoughts. Sara's responses successfully distracted Bill from the topic of their savings account.

The purpose of the misdirection lie is to evade giving a truthful answer to a legitimate question.

The "It Looks Like I Am Giving You an Answer, but I Will Not" Lie

In this pattern of evasion, the respondent again does not give an honest answer to a question, but he or she makes it look like he or she is trying to do so. The following are examples of the unspoken strategy of not answering a question such as, "What did you do today?" or "Do you love me?"

"If you ask me what I did today, I will answer with what I did a week ago. I will act like I am honestly answering your question, but I will keep talking about things that I did all of the days in the week, except for what I did today. I will talk like this until I see that I have successfully distracted you so that you are not interested in a direct answer anymore or forget what you asked me in the first place because I really don't want to tell you what I did today."

Another version is:

"If you ask me if I love you, I will go into a description of what a sweet, accomplished, and lovable person you are. I will talk like that until I see in your eyes that you believe that I love you or until something happens to interrupt my talking to you (like the phone ringing, which I am hoping it will do as I continue to talk). I talk like this because I really don't want to tell you that I love you, because I don't love you, but it serves my purpose to make you think I love you and to keep you hanging around."

This type of lie leaves the person who asked the question feeling that the respondent was genuinely trying to answer. The elaborate, flattering words are not seen as evasive in nature, as they should be. Instead, the listener interprets the words as signs of love and devotion. So the person believes that the respondent loves them, even though the words were never said.

Some politicians use this strategy to evade answering tough questions. They act like they are trying to answer a question, when really they just talk around a topic until the time allotted by interviewers is all used up.

People who lie like this fear the consequences of an honest answer.

The "Behaviors Do Not Match the Words" Lie

Has anyone ever promised to meet you somewhere, confirmed the time and the place of the meeting, and then did not show up? How about when someone says they love you but spends most of their time with someone else? What is going on?

Contradictions between what someone says and what someone does can mean any or all of the following:

- The person is poorly organized, has a short attention span, and/ or is easily distracted from what they told you they would do. If this is the case, you can also see the poor organization in how they run their household, manage their finances, and live their lives.

- The person may want to meet you but feels insecure or unprepared to do so in some way. For example, some people lie because they are hiding a secret.

- The person does not want to see you or be seen with you but does not know how to tell you.

- The person does not want to see you, but saying so would make them look bad. So they act in an upsetting way toward you so that you are justified not seeing them again. They anticipate that you will be angry and hurt enough to break up with them. Since a breakup results in you not seeing each other again, the other person gets what they want: they don't have to be with you. They can even project themselves as the victim of the breakup and blame you: "I don't know what went wrong, he just got mad and broke up with me!"

The lie is that the person will not speak the truth. Their actions convey their true intentions. It is a dysfunctional, immature way to communicate.

The Pathological Liar

A pathological liar lies all the time, whether he has to or not and regardless of the consequences. The lying is incessant.

Routine lying is characteristic of several mental disorders, including conduct disorder, antisocial personality disorder, borderline personality disorder, histrionic personality disorder, and narcissistic personality disorder.[19] Googling these disorders will give you more specific information.

However, pathological liars themselves do not necessarily have any of these disorders. So why are some people pathological liars?

Some research focuses on brain abnormalities that may be associated with pathological lying.[20] Studies have cited decreased activity in the thalamus and increased activity in other parts of the brain.[21] Other research notes that people who lie a lot are more manipulative of people, very sensitive about how they are perceived, and sociable but less socialized than others.[22] However, we do not know what causes people to lie all the time.

Some characteristics of pathological liars are:

- Exaggeration of the smallest things

- Lying even when it is easy to tell the truth

- Presenting themselves as charming, often well dressed and well spoken[23]

- Having no anxiety about being caught in a lie

- Never admitting that they have lied

- Frequent one-upping (Whatever someone has done, the liar has done something better or knows someone who has.)

- The liar's stories change in parts or whole over time because they say whatever they think will impress their audience of the moment and forget what they said in the past.

- The liar believes what he is saying, but nobody who knows them does. The liar cannot remember all of the lies they told, but people who have known them long enough remember very well.

- If you tell them that you do not believe them, they get mad, may fly into a rage, and hang up on you. The next time you see them, they act as though nothing happened.

- Because the liar does not know what honesty is, they also do not know what loyalty is. So watch what you say in their company. The liar will not only broadcast your information, but also will twist and embellish it. Whoever the liar wants to impress will hear about your business.

Whenever you ask a simple question and do not get a simple answer, be on your guard. People lie many ways. Remember this as you are looking for a mate and using your screening criteria.

Your Safeguards Against Lies and Liars

What can you do to keep people from lying to you? The answer, regrettably, is nothing. You have little or no control over what other people say. However, you can guard against believing the lies you are told.

While it can be hard to detect liars, you can develop safeguards against believing lies. Your best defense is to take your time in getting to know people, do background checks, and ask for the opinions of friends and family. Family and friends may identify a liar more quickly than you can.

Most people make the mistake of wishing and thinking that someone is truthful when they are not. When you are looking for someone to marry, you simply cannot indulge in wishful thinking. For this reason, you should never automatically trust anyone you just met.

Your trust needs to be earned with time. You have to spend the time it takes to get to know someone better. The following safeguards should help you in the process.

Do Not Assume that People Always Say the Truth

Most of us believe what we are told and trust people right away. And because most people say the truth the majority of the time, we easily fall into the error of believing a liar.

We also tend to believe what we are told because truthful people assume that everyone else speaks the truth too. This psychological process is known as the defense mechanism of projection. Truthful people subconsciously project their own truthfulness onto other people and tend to believe everything they are told. Liars take advantage of such people, with the result that truthful people often make costly relationship mistakes because they believe the lies they are told.

In therapy I help clients understand how such projection works against them. By being too trusting, many clients have allowed themselves to be hurt. I explain how to adjust their trusting views so they remain a little skeptical. Being a little suspicious is good protection until you have proof of a person's truthful nature.

Do Not Get Emotionally Involved Too Early

Another safeguard against liars is to be mentally aware of the role emotions play in a relationship. This safeguard is your understanding that it is easier to unmask a liar if you are only a casual acquaintance with them. Once you become emotionally involved, your thinking is less clear. Once you are emotionally involved, you may actually join with the liar and make excuses for their deceit.

Therefore, guard your heart. Wait to become emotionally involved until a person's truthfulness has been proven to you.

Check Out All Information You Are Given

A very important safeguard is that you routinely check information you are given. Being cautious early on is better than having regrets later. This is especially true when the information you need is easily obtained.

In the following interview segment, I am counseling a client to do a background check on a woman he just met and already likes. I am advising this because Robert is trusting by nature and people sometimes take advantage of him. Robert and I had several conversations already. At this point, he hesitates to take my advice.

"Robert, you are careful with your money and through hard work saved one hundred and seventy-five thousand dollars." Knowing that he prized his financial accomplishments, I summarized his assets. "That is quite the accomplishment. You've invested in certificates of deposit. You earmarked this money to start your own business someday."

"That's my plan," Robert says and smiles as he thinks of his money. "But what does this have to do with Cindy?"

"I'm coming to that. For your future spouse—be it Cindy or someone else—it would be in your best interest if that woman were good with money too. Now, you can shake your head at this, but just how happy would you be if after the marriage you found out that she has a huge credit card debt? Or that she's in bankruptcy? Or that she is a shopaholic who wants to use your credit cards? Or all three rolled into one? There are lots of people like that. Would it not make sense to find out how Cindy is with money? Also, knowing that sometimes people lie, wouldn't you like to know if she is telling the truth or not?"

"That makes sense. I will have to do a little checking." Robert nods and tries to convince himself of the wisdom of checking. "I shouldn't marry anyone who's bad with money. We would just be arguing all the time. I would be on pins and needles whenever she went to shop online or up to the mall. I would rather not marry at all."

"Here's the bottom line," I continue, seeing that Robert is still struggling with the topic. "If you don't check things out and the person you marry gets you into a mess, shame on you. The information was there for you to research; you just did not bother to reach out for it. You were too busy finding reasons to not do it."

"Yeah, I see your point, Doctor. But for the sake of argument, what if I didn't have that one hundred and seventy-five thousand dollars to protect?"

Good question.

"What about your emotions, your time? You have those to protect, don't you? You still want to check out a person's history. Has she been divorced before? How many times? How is her health? What kinds of medicines does she take? What kind of a family mental health history is there? If you married her and had children, what kind of genes would she be passing on? No one is perfect, but it would be nice to have some idea as to what you are getting into."

I see that Robert is listening, so I continue. "Let me ask the question another way, Robert. What kind of monetary value would you put on your own welfare and mental health?"

In the end, Robert decided to check Cindy's background. He was very pleased to find that Cindy had good credit, little debt, and appeared to be wise with money.

Ways to Do the Checking

Helpful information is right at your fingertips. From your home computer or portable device, you can access all kinds of information. You just need to find the right public information database, be it federal, state, county, or local. You can also pay a nominal fee for online service to do the background checking for you. All you need to do is search.

For example, do you want to know if someone is a licensed barber, plumber, electrician, social worker, psychologist, psychiatrist, doctor, etc., as opposed to posing as one? Log onto your state's Board of Registry of professionals and search.

Do you want to know if someone was ever charged with being a disorderly person, assault and battery, liquor law violations, operating a vehicle after their registration was suspended, etc.? Log onto your state's public safety site and its criminal systems board. Search.

Do you want to know who owns a piece of land or property and what taxes they pay on it? Log onto the city or town's site and look for the address.

Do you want to know what sex offenders live in your area? Log onto your state government's public safety board where you get a description of every level three sex offender.

Do you want a background check on someone but don't have the time to do it? Google the words "find people," and web businesses will offer to do your work for you. The typical background check will offer you an address history; names of relatives; and criminal, marriage, divorce, bankruptcy, death, and other records—all of it public information. The accuracy of the report depends on whether your input information is correct.

Clients often ask me about CORI. This is the Criminal Offender Record Information (CORI), which is a record of person's criminal court appearance in state or federal court. Even if the case is dismissed or if the person is found not guilty, the record remains. Passing a CORI check is necessary to be hired for teaching, day care, public safety and other positions. Landlords double-check a prospective tenant's background using this system. The CORI system can be accessed through the Internet.

If you do not feel like doing the checking yourself at all, a private investigator may be able, with information as limited as a car license plate number, to gather a great deal of information for you. This service tends to be expensive.

Finally, trusted family members and friends can do the checking. Sometimes they are your best choice and source of information. They are your best choice because they love you and have a vested interest in your happiness. It is also because they may have the right connections to get background information. For example, your Uncle Fred is good friends with someone who works at the same company that employs a man you may want to date. Uncle Fred can ask his friend what this man is like on the job, what kind of a worker he is, how well he is liked, etc. In this manner, Uncle Fred can provide you with important information you may not otherwise get. Finally, family members and friends can meet and personally evaluate the person you are interested in. Friends and family members often notice characteristics about a person that you did not but that directly relate to your screening criteria.

The information you need to safeguard yourself is easy to get; use all the resources available to you.

Consulting the Ex of the Person you Like

Sometimes the best safeguard is to talk to the ex. When I think a client of mine could benefit from it, I recommend that he or she contact the ex of the person he or she is seeing. Interviewing exes can be very helpful for the following reasons:

- So my client has some idea as to what kind of a person had a relationship with their loved one before them

- So my client can gather information, such as why the relationship failed from the ex's point of view

- To check out other kinds of important information

I only suggest such a consultation when I am concerned that my client may be making a big mistake. For example, if a girlfriend told my male client that she divorced two husbands because they cheated on her, this may or may not be true. What if she is hard to get along with? What if she cheated on them instead but is lying to look good? You do not know what really happened unless you have the other side's story.

Initially, clients are reluctant to take this step. The ones who do (see Donna in the chapter entitled "Is it a Lie or is it not a Lie?") typically feel that their effort was worthwhile.

Discuss Contradictory Information

Sometimes there is contradictory information about a person. If this is the case, I advise that you discuss the inconsistency. Use the complex, open-ended types of questions mentioned in chapter three. Your raising the questions and the discussion that follows can serve many purposes:

- If there is a good reason for the discrepancy, the person can explain it and all is well again.

- You get to see how the person handles the pressure of being confronted.

- You may get an answer if the person was lying or not.

- If after the confrontation you believe that the person lied to you, think back to how they did it originally and whether you could detect if it happened again, thereby learning to detect lying better.

- You gain experience in talking about uncomfortable topics with another person.

For your safety and comfort, conduct such discussions in a public place with people around. That way you are less likely to get angry outbursts. Or, if the other party becomes overly agitated or belligerent, it is easier to exit the situation.

Keep Observing, Keep Thinking

The last safeguard is to look for clues that people give about themselves. These clues are there for all to observe and recognize, but people miss them because they do not think about what they mean.

For example, people drop clues in how they behave toward others and maintain their possessions. Observe and think about the following[24]:

- What does the person's car look like? What is the state and condition of the vehicle? Is it taken care of? Is it registered and insured? Is there clutter in the vehicle? How much clutter is there and how long has it been there? Is it a flashy car? Is it too expensive for what the person's income is?

- Is the person on time for work and appointments? Do they pay their bills and get things done on time?

- What are the person's associates and friends like? How comfortable are you with them?

- Do family members ever call? How does the person act toward their parents and family?

- Is the person patient and respectful or abrupt and impatient? Are you ever mentioned in the telephone call? Does the person sometimes later tell you what the call was about, so as to make you feel included?

- How does this person act when they are tired or frustrated? Is this a person you want to be with when the car breaks down on the highway? People really show who they are when they are tired and do not have the energy to hold a façade together. In other words, if you really want to see what a person is made of, observe them in a frustrating situation.

- Does the person treat you well, consistently? Is the person telling you what you want to hear or what they really think? Keep asking yourself these questions over time.

- How does the person talk about previous relationships? Are they respectful about the people they loved before you, or is their speech accusatory and abusive?

Remember what you have observed and discovered through background checks. This is who the person is. Does the person meet your screening criteria?

In this chapter you learned how to safeguard yourself against lies. You also now know to double-check the truthfulness of information you receive. These are things in your control; they are things you can do to protect yourself as you go about finding a mate.

There is something else in your control as well. You do have a choice about how you present yourself to people. Maybe there is something you can to do improve your self-presentation. Read the next chapter; then decide for yourself.

6

ꝋꝋꝋꝋ

PRESENTING YOURSELF TO FUTURE MATES

You never get a second chance
to make a first impression.

Will Rogers,
American humorist

So far we have discussed the use of safeguards and how to tell if someone is lying. Another important part of meeting people is your self-presentation.

You realize, of course, that while you are evaluating people to see if they meet your criteria, they are probably doing the same to you. They will ask you questions about yourself. You need to be ready to answer and present yourself well. Your goal is to make a good impression.

Self-Preparation

How can you make a good impression? Let's start by reviewing how you present yourself. Ask yourself the following questions:

- What are my strengths and weaknesses? How well can I talk about them if someone asks me?

- How do I interact with people? How could I do it better?

- When someone asks about me, do I relax and give a good response?

- How do I talk about myself? Is my attitude positive? Does it show?

- Do I realize that what I say may be repeated to others? Can I be tight-lipped if need be?

- Am I always courteous and honest?

- Do I pay a reasonable amount of attention to my appearance? Am I reasonably neat and healthy-looking?

- Do I dominate conversations? Do I boast? Do I belittle myself?

Your answers to these questions are important. Use them to improve how you present yourself.

Common Mistakes in Self-Presentation

1. You present yourself as too self-assured and self-centered. Do you act entitled? Are you aware of it? It may not be your fault. People who are naturally relaxed, excel at academics or sports, and/or are financially comfortable often appear self-centered without meaning to. The disadvantage is that this comfort with yourself might be perceived as your being self-centered, arrogant or entitled.

   Some people act entitled because they believe the world, their parents, or someone else owes them something. Is this you? Is your entitled presentation the reason why people express an initial interest in you but do not pursue further contact?

2. You present yourself as bashful. If you cannot make small talk, if you cannot communicate your feelings and ideas, you have a problem and you need to fix it. The problem with being a shy person is that other people may interpret your bashfulness as your being aloof, unapproachable, and (ironically enough) arrogant—yes, just as though you were self-centered and entitled.

   Sometimes you need to make small talk because you need to signal that you are approachable and that you take an interest in the other person. The ability to make limited small talk is a necessary social tool. If you struggle making small talk, try using the mnemonic device LIFE mentioned in chapter three.

3. You present yourself as odd, different. Your physical presentation is off. Your clothing, speech, behavior, or accessories signal something negative. In general, any extreme clothing, body odor, attitude, or extensive body art such as piercings, tattoos, etc., invite people to make immediate judgments about you.

4. You present yourself as sexy, flashy, or rich. You dress to show off your body. You drive expensive cars and carry gadgets to show off your money. Again, you are hurting yourself. Why? Isn't it great to be rich or beautiful? It can be. But remember your goal. You do not want someone attracted to you for your body or your money because then they may overlook the real you. Furthermore, you foolishly created the situation through your self-presentation so people like you precisely for the assets you advertised but not for you as a person.

You want just the opposite. You want to be wanted and loved for yourself. That is why you want to present yourself in a way that people will to get to know you. Do not let your entitled attitude, bashful social skills, odd presentation, or good looks and riches get in the way of your goal of getting to know people and people getting to know you.

What Do You Need to Change?

Take a minute to review your self-presentation. If you have no idea as to what kind of impression you make, ask people to tell you. Trusted family members, friends, clergy, or coaches will give you accurate feedback, especially if they realize that you want to know. Their advice may be one or more of the following:

- You need to change your attitude somehow: from sour to contented, from being too shy to being more outgoing, from acting too entitled/cocky to acting more humble, or something else.

- You need to change your appearance and speech: how you dress, how you talk, how you maintain eye contact, how well and cleanly you speak, how to talk less if you tend to dominate conversations, and how to talk more if you are shy, or something else.

- You need to change by developing yourself into a better person. Maybe you have been told that you need to stop drinking or using drugs, start and finish training and schooling, get a job, stop spending, pay off your debts, lose weight, act nicer to the people who love you, pay attention to your personal hygiene, or something else.

Make the change. By becoming a better person, you will feel better about yourself. People will notice that you are comfortable with yourself and be attracted to you because of it.

It is in your interest to listen to feedback about how you present yourself. It is in your interest to use the feedback to change for the better.

Changing Your Self-Presentation

Changing for the better is change worth making for its own sake. A change for the better can also create better social opportunities for you to find a spouse. Is it worth it to you? If your answer is yes, here is how you can go about changing:

First, you need to want to change and decide what to change. Will you change your style, your substance, or both?

Second, if you are not sure how to go about changing, get some help. Ask trusted people for guidance. A good therapist can also help.

Third, because change does not come easily, you need to be determined to work at it. For example, if you decide to become better at public speaking, it will take several efforts to master this skill. Stay self-disciplined. Whatever your goal is, practice the new presentation and behaviors. Do not give up.

Fourth, if change is hard for you, try professional assistance. Professional counselors can help people to change where possible. They can help you present yourself better, practice your social skills, and address other concerns. If you decide to go this route, make sure you like the counselor as a person. It is okay to shop around until you find someone you like, only check with your health insurance to see if it will pay for it. Your health insurance often pays for the cost of psychotherapy by licensed mental health professionals (Please see Appendix B for a listing of the different types of counselors).

Fifth, improving yourself has two great rewards. The first reward is tangible: you will get to know more people and thus will be more likely to meet someone who meets your screening criteria for a no-divorce marriage.

The second reward is that you will be proud of yourself for the self-improvements you've made. This is the pride that comes from having worked toward a goal and having won your objective. This is the kind of pride that builds your self-confidence.

Finally, the ability to change for the better is a desirable personal asset. One positive change can lead to others, precisely because you have demonstrated to yourself that you can do it. Desirable marriage partners value this ability.

Presenting Your Disadvantages

Some people have checkered pasts. This means that they engaged in activities that resulted in sexually transmitted diseases, various addictions, serious medical conditions, financial problems, gambling, drinking and drug issues, troubles with the law, poor family and interpersonal relationships, multiple marriages, and so forth.

People with such problems realize that they are less-than-desirable marriage material. Because they fear rejection, they do not talk about their pasts and problems. If anything, they cover up the past.

Some people never admit their problems unless forced to do so. Others disclose information if they think they are in a safe relationship and their partner will forgive their transgressions. That is why many confessions are made (and previously self-contained behaviors become visible) two weeks before a wedding or soon after it.

It does not have to be that way. There are better ways of facing the past.

When clients raise their checkered pasts in therapy, it is usually because their conscience is bothering them. I take this as a sign of health because not everybody has a conscience. The need to confess the past is positive; it signals the client's need to talk and maybe make retribution for the past. Talking about a troubling past can lead to a better future. Here are some examples:

Example A: "Doc, I am happy that I am getting married soon. But I am really worried too. I was stupid in the past. Do I have to tell my fiancé about my abortion(s)? I feel like I should."

Example B: "I told her I only *used* Valium. I never told her I am dealing too. It bothers me some, even though I make good money doing it. Does she need to know I am dealing? Or maybe I should stop using and dealing both. I don't know. I've thought of going straight before; this is not how I was raised. What do you think, Doc? Can I do it? Also what should I tell her and how?"

Example C: "I've had herpes for years. I can control it. I wash the bed sheets every night. He wonders why. Should I come clean with him? I don't want to have secrets from him."

Example D: "All of a sudden I am thirty thousand dollars in debt. I guess I was spending a lot the last few months. I just got engaged, and my fiancée asked if I have a lot of debt. What is a lot? How can I handle this?"

Example E: "I told my girlfriend that I was going to court for child support. But I was really going about my role in a breaking and entering charge. I feel bad about lying to her. By the way, Doc, don't worry; I am never going to break into your office. You're not worried now, are you? I am a really good person; I was just stupid. But my girlfriend, is she going to find out that I lied by reading the paper? How do I make it right?"

Honesty Is the Best Policy

Being honest is the only way to get rid of a guilty conscience. Being honest about what you did wrong is an exercise in personal responsibility. It brings you closer to make things right. Other benefits of saying the truth are:

- You are no longer stressing yourself by keeping your past behavior a secret.

- You face what you have done, take responsibility for it, and make restitution.

- You get to describe the context of your bad choices.

- Your listener is able to ask questions and may value your sincerity.

- You may have a chance to point out how far you have come since your past errors.

- You may be granted forgiveness.

- Your listener is not hearing a worse version of your past from someone else.

- Your listener does not find out about your past by doing a background check and conclude that you willfully deceived him/her.

The last point is particularly important. A checkered past is not easy to hide anymore. As I noted in the last chapter, there is public information about you that can be easily accessed. For example, if you are telling people that you have been divorced only once when in fact it has been three or four times, that information can be found by anyone interested in doing a little research.

Or if you are calling yourself a registered nurse, a plumber, a doctor, an attorney, or any other professional entity, someone can easily check to see if you indeed are that and also whether any complaints have been made against you. Private investigators can find even more information.

There are two major disadvantages to telling the truth. The first is that you might lose the person you love. The second is that your past may be told to others. Whether either happens depends upon the seriousness of your past failings and the character of the person you love. There is always the chance, however, that the person you love decides to forgive and continue loving you.

The clients in Examples A through E all decided to talk about their pasts. They asked me to help them find the words to best deliver their message. They wanted to stay calm and respectful, no matter how their loved one reacted. Due to space limitations,

I will only describe how Jill, my client from Example A, revealed her abortions and handled her fiancée's reaction.

Role-Play in Therapy:
Presenting Shocking Information to a Fiancée

Role-playing is a psychotherapy technique that helps clients practice difficult conversations they expect to have. It is a relatively simple but very helpful technique. Most of the time, the client asks the therapist to play the role of the beloved person. The role-play exercise continues until the client feels ready for the real-life conversation.

Jill (from Example A) wanted to tell Jim about her abortions. A long time before meeting him, Jill drank and made poor choices. Now Jill was sober, against abortion, and delighted to be marrying Jim. As her happiness escalated, her conscience began to bother her. She felt that she had done terrible things in the past. She just couldn't keep it to herself; she had to tell Jim. She wanted to say what she did, ask for forgiveness, and face the consequences. She wanted me to role-play Jim.

"Jim," Jill said to me, "I am sorry that I have withheld something from you. I would like to tell you about it now."

"What is it, honey?" was my (and Jim's anticipated) reply.

"Well, it is something that has weighed on me for some time. It was stuff that went on during my college years."

"There's nothing you can't tell me; we're getting married."

"I know, and I am very happy about that. But maybe because I love you so much, I feel guilty. I have thought about it, and I want to tell you."

"So tell me."

"You know my views on abortion, Jim. I feel that an embryo is a person and that abortion is wrong. I know that you agree with me on that. But there was a time, when I was young and careless, that I did not think at all. Looking back on it, I have a hard time believing that I really had abortions. But I did have them, Jim."

There is stunned silence from Jim. Jill continues to talk.

"I finally got up the courage to face myself. I had a big debate with myself. And I felt that I had to tell you. I am truly sorry for the pain and the shock of it to you."

I (Jim) looked as though a car just hit me. Jim finally says, "I am going to have to think about this."

This was the first part. Jill and I next role-played possible follow-up conversations that might result from the first one. Again, I am playing the role of Jim, who is quite upset.

"Why didn't you tell me sooner? Why are you telling me two months before the wedding?"

"I don't know. Something stirred inside me. I just couldn't withhold this from you. I love you, and I feel that I can't marry you without telling you."

"Fine timing there!" Jim yells in exasperation. "Now, if I wanted to, we couldn't call off the wedding."

"Jim, of course we can call off the wedding. I understand that you might want to. If that is your decision, we will do that."

"You had this all figured out ahead of time."

"It has been eating away at me for a while. I went to talk to a therapist. Then I thought, well, if I were Jim, how would I take this news? I realized that you might not want me anymore, but I was hoping you still would."

"By the way, how many abortions were there, and with how many men?"

"There were five abortions in all, with three men involved. I was very stupid. I was drinking, and I did not think. I wish I could change the past if even for just myself."

Jim's pain erupted from him. He had to take time to settle himself. He next said, "So what does the doctor say? Can you still have babies?"

"I asked the doctor. I am fine. I can have babies."

"I want to hear that from the doctor herself."

"I understand that. I will call her to make an appointment. I will sign a consent form so she can release my medical information and discuss it with you."

"And I don't know about the wedding. I may call it off."

"I understand. It's my fault. I am truly sorry for the pain I caused you."

This was a tough one. It took a lot of role-playing for Jill to choose the words that best conveyed her meaning. At the same time, because she truly loved Jim, she was hurting about having to hurt him.

She realized she should have raised her past earlier in the relationship. She also realized that if she had a right to be angry, it was only at herself for being reckless and irresponsible in the past. She tried to prepare herself for Jim saying that the wedding was off and their relationship over. I could see that she feared the worst.

Jill's maturity, genuine regret, and respectful attitude toward Jim eventually carried the relationship forward. The gynecologist met with Jim and repeated her opinion that Jill should have no trouble carrying and delivering babies. After a while, Jim was able to appreciate how hard it was for his bride to be honest on a matter that she was ashamed of and could have kept concealed. With time, Jim valued her honesty all the more. He forgave Jill. The wedding did take place a year after originally planned.

Use of Internet and Professional Dating Services

Many of my clients and acquaintances use online and professional dating services. There is nothing shameful about using them, although they are not for everyone. Most people find online services easy to use, relatively inexpensive, and resulting in at least a few dates. I know many people who met their spouses this way.

The safeguards described in chapters four and five are extremely important, especially protecting your private information from Internet abuse. Remember, you are meeting complete strangers online, not friends of friends. It is important that you look out for your safety. The more expensive, personalized professional dating services typically conduct background checks on all participants while the less expensive, Internet-based ones do not. Either way, you travel at your own risk. The risk is greater with inexpensive online services.

The low cost of Internet dating is attractive to many people. Electronic socializing from the comfort of one's home is a major advantage. Busy professional people and single parents who cannot get out of the house in the evening hours like the convenience.

On the other hand, professional dating services appeal to people who are very busy, have money, and must protect their privacy. Although these services are much more expensive, they can save money on the long run. One of my money-conscious clients documented the advantage of paying over $4,000 to an exclusive dating service and explained how this investment was going to save him money.

"I did some calculations, Dr. O'Hara," he told me one day, pulling a piece of paper with numbers out of his pocket. "It is very expensive to be single and going out, year after year.

"Here's what I figured," he continued. "Let's say I am on a less expensive online dating service. If I go out once or twice a week to meet someone, it will cost me somewhere between ten dollars to one hundred dollars a week. Doing the math, that is a minimum of five hundred and twenty to five thousand and two hundred dollars a year spent on drinks, food, and minimal entertainment."

My client looked at his paper again and said, "If I want to go to a theater, movies, or baseball games, I could easily spend one hundred and fifty to three hundred dollars a week or seven thousand and eight hundred to fifteen thousand and six hundred dollars a year. I can't spend that, of course, but I calculated to see how expensive dating could get over time. Let's say I spend one hundred and fifty dollars a week for the five more years that I may be single; that amounts to thirty-nine thousand dollars. If I only spend one hundred dollars a week, that is twenty-six thousand dollars for five years. If I spend ten dollars a week, which is just about the life of a hermit meeting a woman for a cup of coffee once a week, then over five years I have paid out two thousand and six hundred dollars."

My client concluded, "If I did the less expensive online dating search for another five years, it could cost me as much as the down-payment on a house! Besides, I don't want to search and spend. It would be easier, and maybe less expensive, to hire a higher end dating service. My chances of finding my match may be better and cheaper that way anyway."

Besides trying to save money, this client also valued his time and privacy. Using the more expensive dating service, he did not have to post anything on the Web. The service did the searching, the background checks, the matching. There were no e-mails exchanged. The service gave my client the phone number of a woman to call. She answered, and they arranged to meet.

The majority of people I know search online. There are many sites to seek people, so I recommend that if you choose to search online, you select the service which best meets your personal needs.

By reading this chapter, you have probably learned how to present yourself well. However, you may be a person who believes that you have very little good to present about yourself. If so, I have met and worked with people like you. You feel that you have too many disadvantages. You feel that it would take a miracle for you to have a happy marriage.

The next chapter is written for you. In it, I describe how one person overcame his disadvantages.

7

ꙮ

How You Can Overcome Disadvantages

If you hope,
There's a rope,
And climb that rope
You can.

Christina S. O'Hara

In the last chapter, we discussed how to present yourself to your best advantage when meeting people. I believe that most everyone can present themselves to good advantage. Everyone has some good traits to present. Unfortunately, some people disagree. They feel that there is nothing good about themselves. They believe that if they ever marry, their marriage will end in divorce.

They feel ashamed of their family histories. Many come from dysfunctional families where divorce is frequent and normal. Others have alcohol and drug abuse histories and feel that just staying sober and abstinent is a struggle.

If this is how you feel, this chapter is written for you. I have met you. You come into my office and say you want to be happy.

You don't know what happy feels like, but you want it. You say you dream of marriage, children, and a happy home. You say you have no idea how to make that happen. All you have is the idea of it because you heard about it from other people but you never experienced it yourself.

If you are willing to work at it, you just may get your wish. The ability to change for the better is a remarkable human trait. Your motivation to improve your life is the starting point. You start at the starting point and trust that there is a finish line somewhere. My job is to assist you in getting to the finish line. It is also my honor and pleasure to accompany clients who wish to build a better life.

Overcoming Alcohol Abuse and a Dysfunctional Family Background

I could write volumes about how many of my clients overcame personal problems and family backgrounds. Space limitations restrict me to Mark's case. This is the story of a computer technician who changed from drinking to sobriety and recovery and eventually became a happy person. It was a new sensation for him to enjoy life. Because of these self-improvements, he eventually attracted the type of woman he wanted to marry.

Mark appeared very uncomfortable when he first walked into my office. He barely sat down; he was precariously balanced on the edge of his seat. I thought that at any moment he would leap to his feet and run away.

"What brings you in, Mark?"

"I've had a touch of trouble with alcohol, Doc," he said, shifting uneasily but looking right at me. He was probably wondering how a petite, middle-aged, female psychologist could help him.

"What kind of trouble?"

"Well, actually, a lot of trouble. I'm here seeing you because I was court-ordered to come." At this point Mark let out a big breath, and his shoulders drooped. He looked miserable.

"Please tell me everything about it," I said, and I meant it. In every case, I need to know the details in order to best assist. If the client leaves out something important, we might find ourselves wasting time and effort.

Mark took the leap. He let out a big breath. "I'll start at the beginning. My folks are alcoholics. There was a lot of trouble in my family, and I swore I would never drink. I was pretty good for a while. But then I got drunk at a party, got behind the wheel, got stopped, and now have a DUI on my record."

Mark's presentation sounded honest and well organized. As he described the details of that evening, he appeared genuinely sorry for the mess he had gotten into. That was now, with a probation officer on his back. What would happen later? How motivated was he to stop drinking?

"How do you think I might be able to assist you, Mark?"

"I want you to help me stop drinking. I want to stop altogether."

After finishing the intake interview I said, "Okay. I'll try to help you the best I can."

It was not easy for Mark to be in therapy with me. I'm the kind of therapist who does not waste people's time. I move the therapy process along as quickly as people can take it. I saw that Mark moved right along.

As time went on, Mark joined Alcoholics Anonymous, got a sponsor, and started the steps. He learned to understand his triggers to drink and developed strategies to combat them. He stayed sober and started recovery work. He accepted God as his higher power and started going to church. He learned to socialize without alcohol, found friends who did not drink, and even socialized in settings where alcohol was present but did not drink.

Once the court-mandated therapy sessions and probationary period for his DUI were satisfied, I wondered what Mark would do. Many people leave therapy at this time because they think they no longer need it. But Mark did not leave. As I found out, he was just getting started.

"Okay, Doc. For someone not in AA, you have proven yourself to me. You're okay," he said one day. "I want you to help me with something even more difficult."

There are few things in life more difficult than staying sober when you have a strong alcoholic genetic background. But people are full of surprises, so I was bracing myself for a heavy revelation such as, *"Well, I am addicted to cocaine as well, only I didn't tell you that just yet."* But that was not it.

"Doc, I realize that alcoholism is in my genes and that I will be passing it onto my children," Mark explained. "I want my kids to have a chance, so I really would like to marry someone without an alcohol background. Someone who is not an alcoholic or adult child of an alcoholic (ACOA)."

He continued, "My dream is to have a peaceful household. My dream is to make a home where there is no fighting and screaming so that my children can relax and not cringe with fear the way I did when I was a kid. I want to read stories to them and cuddle on the couch. Stuff like that."

Mark's faced tensed as he said, "But here is my worry. What nice woman would want me? Me from a family like I come from? Someone like me with a DUI? Me, an AA member for life?"

Then Mark came to the point. "Since you are not an alcoholic, Doc, I thought that maybe you could point me in the right direction. I want to know how non-alcoholic people live and feel. You could teach me about that. Maybe I could move beyond where I am, you know? What do you think?"

Not often does an alcoholic ask like this, at least not in such a precise manner. An alcoholic usually marries another alcoholic or an ACOA. This happens because people who drink form their own social groups, which excludes light social or non-drinkers. The heavy drinking group limits the social development of their members because all socializing happens under the influence. For this reason, heavy drinkers do not learn the social skills or problem-solving methods that light social or non-drinkers do. Heavy drinkers limit their social options to other drinkers and ACOAs who have learned to live with them.

It is uncomfortable for ACOAs and alcoholics to date non-alcoholics. Children raised in alcoholic families were not the focus of love, attention, and appropriate guidance. Children growing up in alcoholic families struggle through life by being caretakers, acting out, or emotionally shutting down. On the other hand, children raised in child-centered, orderly homes are generally more confident, better socialized, and emotionally more capable than ACOAs or alcoholics. That is why people with these different backgrounds are not attracted to each other. Alcoholics and ACOAs typically will not date people raised sober, whom they consider cocky or too happy. When it comes time to date and marry, ACOAs and alcoholics pick their own kind.

Mark understood this and wanted to break the cycle. Marrying someone from a non-alcoholic household was a step forward for him, and he wanted to make it his life goal.

Of course I would assist him. Mark had hope that he could change; now he needed the rope to climb. We added new treatment goals. The new goals were for Mark to develop himself as a person, to socialize more, to establish his acceptance and rejection criteria, to become comfortable with himself, and to marry and have a happy household.

"Mark, of course I'll try to help, but I need to tell you it won't be easy," I said. "It is not as simple as finding a woman without an alcohol history. You need to be happy with yourself first. Then you hope to meet a woman who is stable all around." When

Mark asked what I meant by that, I continued, "She needs to be mentally healthy in other ways too if you would like a happy household. You would not want her to be bipolar or anything like that."

Mark thought it over. "Yes, I agree. Look, Doc, I know this is a long shot for me, but I want to try to find someone wholesome. I want a happy family. I am willing to work for it."

"Well, let's get started. How about we start with developing your own set of acceptance and rejection screening criteria? In the process of that we might touch upon the other goals you set for therapy."

Mark worked through establishing acceptance and rejection screening criteria. He socialized with AA friends and a non-AA friend from work. He was ready to meet women, but I noticed that the way he presented himself showed that he was uncomfortable with himself. Was there something he had not told me?

I decided to comment on his apparent discomfort. "Mark, I understand that you want a happier family than the one you came from. So far your major concern is the alcoholism, the DUI, and your family background. Is there anything else that I should know about? Maybe something you have not mentioned to me?"

"No, Doc. No other drugs." Mark was reading my mind. "No sexually transmitted diseases. My general health is good. I have steady work. I got a promotion at work, and I can pay my bills. I can't think of anything else that is really bad about me."

"Do you have any children out of wedlock? Paternity payments? Bankruptcies? Debt? A gambling habit? Legal proceedings against you? Anything like that?" I had already asked these questions in my initial diagnostic interview, but asking again seemed like a good idea.

Mark replied, looking straight at me, "No. I just feel insecure. I have so little self-confidence. I think a nice woman will just laugh at me."

I was relieved. The absence of all that "bad stuff" was important. I would use it as a therapeutic tool. I could use the absence of bad stuff to get Mark to awaken to the good things about himself. I started suggesting to Mark that the absence of bad stuff was, in reality, a good situation. It showed that he had some strengths, but he needed to own them.

To move forward, Mark would need to recognize these good things about himself, take ownership of them, and learn to talk more positively about himself. This was the psychological road to reach his new therapeutic goals. If and when Mark traveled this road, I thought he might attain at least some of his goals.

Developing a Good Attitude and Talking Positively

"You lost me, Doc. What is this about the absence of bad stuff being good?"

"I'm sorry, Mark. I probably wasn't clear enough. Here's what I suggest," I said, opening a new psychological venue, "let's make a list of all of the good things about you."

"Doc, you must be joking."

"I am very serious. Besides, how many times have you heard me joke about important things?"

"Well, I mean, that is just the problem. I don't have any positives about me. I certainly don't have any to attract a decent woman."

"Let us just see, shall we? Didn't you tell me you got a promotion at work?"

Now began the work to get Mark to see himself positively. He was so painfully aware of his shortcomings that he struggled to see himself in a positive light. At first he was defensive about changing what he thought of himself. My job was to work through his defensive network. I decided to quicken the process by laying out my plan.

"Here's what I am thinking, Mark. Of course, there is your past. But you have done a lot of work to improve yourself. You worked hard in AA, got a sponsor, and are doing the steps and staying sober. That is to your credit. All that struggle and staying sober counts as a strength. It shows that you have some inner strength to change yourself when you have to. Do you have any idea how many people have little or no ability to change? I am sure we both know people like that."

I could see in Mark's eyes that he was considering all this, so I continued, "Another of your strengths is that you are gainfully employed in a useful field and are getting promotions. That is very attractive to a woman who wants a family. You need to see yourself and your job in a positive light. You need to talk about yourself and your job in a positive way."

"Okay. I am just not used to thinking like this," Mark mused. "This is all so weird."

"Well, sure it is. But it is only weird because you are thinking these things for the first time. Once you think them the hundredth time, these positive thoughts about yourself will become natural and comfortable. They will be because they are true."

As time went on, Mark and I made a list of his strengths and attractive qualities. I asked him to read his list several times a day and to make one good comment about himself every day.

One day Mark said, "Sometimes I think I may be happy. It is a strange feeling, even though this is what I want. I keep having to reassure myself that it's okay to be happy."

And then, jokingly, he asked, "I am not getting too conceited here, am I?"

"Not likely." I smiled back. "What you are feeling is normal. This is how non-alcoholic people feel. We are working toward you becoming happy. The type of woman you are looking for feels like this. We are working toward you being able to understand her feelings of happiness and share happy feelings with her."

I continued, "That is how you will connect with the type of woman you are looking for. When she feels happy, it will not feel strange to you. When she says something nice about her family, job, or vacation she's planning, you will not feel like she is bragging about it. You will be able to smile back and feel happy for her because the feeling of happiness will be familiar to you. You are the one that needs to be happy with yourself if you are to have a happy household."

"So it all starts with how I feel about myself. It all starts with my attitude. I need to relax and welcome this weird feeling of happiness." Mark said this very quietly and then looked at the floor.

I let a few moments pass.

Then he said, "So if I'm happy, I can also talk about my past better, I guess."

"Sure. You can say anything with a good attitude," I replied, building on Mark's insight. "You can say to the women you meet that you had a DUI and it woke you up to the fact that you needed to change. You can say that if the police officer never caught you, you would not be where you are today. You can say that because of that DUI, you are actually happier and healthier today than you have ever been in your whole life."

"Yes, I can say that now because it is true."

Mark's eyes had a new light in them as he remarked, "I got lemons when I was born, but I learned to make lemonade, right?"

From this point forward, Mark was more relaxed and started liking himself a little. He was moving higher and higher on that rope he was climbing.

Eventually, Mark met Wendy. Wendy appreciated Mark's emotional accomplishments and that he was earnest in wanting a good life for his family. What Wendy most appreciated was that Mark:

- Recognized the dysfunctional household he grew up in

- Showed sympathy rather than anger toward his parents

- Did not let the past bring him down

- Took responsibility, got help for himself, and worked hard to become a better person

- Wanted a good future

- Was able to change for the better

- Was happy with himself and with others

- Was a hard worker and would be a good provider

Wendy and Mark got married. Today they have three children and are contented with their marriage.

Presenting as a Good Marriage Prospect with a Dysfunctional Background

At first glance, both Mark and Jill (from the last chapter) appear to be poor candidates for marriage. Mark's disadvantages were his chaotic, alcoholic family background and DUI. Jill's were her past drinking, poor choices, and abortions. Both sets of disadvantages could very well keep a potential mate from accepting them in marriage.

However, because of the road they traveled out of their pasts, both Mark and Jill changed for the better as people. Both worked hard to change. Mark had his hopes (for a nice wife and family) to propel his way forward. Jill had her conscience to guide her to be honest and take responsibility for her past actions.

Out of dysfunction and misery, both Mark and Jill were able to build happy lives. Their stories serve to remind us that good marital partners may have dysfunctional pasts. This is not to say that all people with dysfunctional pasts are able to move forward as Mark and Jill did. That is not the case. Mark and Jill were exceptionally insightful and motivated. Many people, even if they do go to therapy, do not make as much progress as they did. But some people can make progress and move on to have fine marriages.

Understanding that Dysfunctional Families May Produce Good Spouses and that Well-Functioning Families May Produce Poor Marital Spouses

Just as a good marriage prospect can emerge from a dysfunctional family background, so can a bad marriage prospect emerge from a healthy family background. Well-functioning couples and families can produce a child that is difficult, unhappy, and full of problems.

Do not assume that just because someone came from an intact, happy, and cohesive family he or she will make a fine spouse for you. First of all, the family may not be as close or happy as what appears. You need to know the family for a while to judge for yourself. It takes time to understand the person's place in their family and what family members think of them.

Approach a person from a good family with as much healthy skepticism as you would someone with a checkered past or poor family background. Ask all the questions you need to determine if that person meets your criteria. Use your safeguards and do background checks. Finally, do not become emotionally involved until your trust has been earned and you've determined that the person is suitable for you to marry them.

Trusted family members can be very helpful to you in many different ways, no matter the type of family you come from. In the next chapter I detail the ways they can help you. I will also comment on how good friends can help in your quest for a good spouse.

8

How Family and Friends Can Help

People often overlook a very important resource: the advice and support of trusted family members and friends. This oversight may be due to people wanting to make their own decisions. Independence of thought and action is the psychological foundation of the American people. Individual freedoms such as the right to the pursuit of happiness are deeply ingrained in our way of thinking.

While this independent streak is admirable, it should not be carried to extremes. Finding a good spouse can be tricky business. If trusted family members and friends offer advice or help, listen up. They have your interest at heart and want to see you happy. Because they love you, they will risk your displeasure at them by telling you something you need to know. If this happens to you, listen up and remember that it is better to be hurt now than to live in misery later.

What follows are some of the ways that family and friends can help. If you are lacking family and friends, experienced mental health providers can assist by helping you understand and evaluate the people you meet. (See Appendix B for a listing of the different types of mental health professionals.)

Helping by Communicating and Listening

Talking: Caring parents stay in emotional contact with their children by spending lots of face-to-face time in joint activities and discussions. As the child grows up, parents do most of the work of communicating and listening during which the child hopefully learns to respect and value parental opinion. This developmental process lays the foundation for later discussions, such as when the grown child is ready to date and marry.

Listening: Family members and friends can help by being sympathetic listeners in times of trouble. A hurt, angry person needs someone to talk to. Family members or friends can help by giving full attention and offering support.

Listen for as long as it takes. If asked, you can mention what you might do in the same situation. Do not try to solve the problem unless requested to do so. In general, the single person learns best if he meets life's challenges on his own, whether it is in consultation with family and friends or not.

Helping by Providing Select Environments

Parents often help their children by immersing them in select environments with approved playmates. The following are examples of how this is done.

Environments Emphasizing Social Class: Children of wealthy parents socialize in select environments with other rich children. Money buys these environments. The parents arrange for their children to attend private schools, invite each other to parties, room together at boarding school and college, and socialize in private clubs. As the children mature, they are instructed about the financial underpinnings of their life-style and the advantages of being around their own kind. They are also taught to marry within their own socio-economic set because not doing so may well result in loss of status, connections, friends, inheritance, and cash flow.

Most of all, rich children grow up learning to guard their emotional security. Rich children who date persons who are not rich often report that they are not sure if they are liked for their assets or for themselves. To decrease the risk of being emotionally exploited (i.e. being pursued and married for their wealth), rich children safeguard themselves by marrying people of their own financial strata.

Environments Emphasizing Religious Affiliations: Some religions are quite strict about whom their members may socialize with and marry. The Jehovah's Witness and Muslim religions come to mind. For example, in the Muslim religion, the Sharia Laws dictate how a Muslim must behave, socialize, and interact with members of other religions. For a Muslim person, there is no separation of church and state, such as exists for Christians, Buddhists, or Jews. For a Muslim to be able to call himself a Muslim, he has to follow the Sharia Laws, some of which are in conflict with mainstream American cultural and legal practices.

In the area of marriage, the Sharia law is explicit. It dictates that a Muslim woman is forbidden to marry a non-Muslim. (If a Christian man wished to marry a Muslim woman, he would have to become a Muslim first.) However, a Muslim man may marry a Christian woman, because it is understood that the Christian woman is subservient to the Muslim husband and that their children will be raised Muslim. In order to be in compliance with these laws, most Muslim parents restrict their children's socializing to other Muslims.

In general, American religions are tolerant of inter-faith marriages, but all prefer same-faith marriages and provide social opportunities for same-faith young people to meet, socialize, and relax. Although children sometimes view their parents' actions as forceful in nature, the parental efforts to promote same-faith marriages are usually full of good intentions. From their own experience, parents realize that being married is not easy and that marrying someone with no religion or from another religion may complicate their child's married life. This is one reason why many parents encourage same-faith marriages.

Environments Emphasizing Abilities such as Athleticism and Academics: Parents of academically and intellectually precocious children often seek environments where such gifts can be enhanced. It is the same for athletically gifted youngsters. The child's advanced ability determines how, when, and with whom the child socializes.

Achievement through these abilities becomes the focal point of adolescent and adult life. Whoever marries the exceptional athlete or intellectual needs to understand, accept, and support the lifestyle associated with their abilities and accomplishment needs.

Helping by Supporting Safety and Information Gathering

Here are some ways your friends can help with safety issues and information collection. Consider the following:

Example A: If you are going someplace new, take along a friend as your witness and helper, just in case something goes wrong. Let the person who invited you know that you will be bringing a friend along.

Example B: If you are meeting someone new (maybe for coffee with someone you met online), ask a friend to call you on your cell phone while you are out. Arrange for a code word you can use in case of trouble. If you use the code word, the friend can create an urgent need for you to come home, send the police, or come to where you are.

Example C: Ask friends to double-check information someone gave you. If a friend grew up nearby where the person you are meeting was raised, ask your friend if they know anything about the person's family or their background.

Example D: Ask your friends what they think of the new person you are seeing. If you are a woman and brought around a new man, ask male friends for their honest opinions. They will give their opinion if they think you really want to know. If you are a man, ask women friends for their impressions of the woman you brought around. Your friends may have noticed things that you have not.

Trusted family members whose opinions you value may also be helpful and protective of your welfare and personal happiness. You can say and ask:

Example E: "Uncle Fred, do you know someone who can do a background check on this lovely lady I just met? She seems really nice, but I just want to make sure she is all she seems to be."

Example F: "Mom and Dad, I'd like to get your opinion on a new man. Do you think you could join us for coffee next weekend? I want to see how this man interacts with you and get your first impressions of him."

Example G: "Aunt Anne, I just met a girl who says she belongs to the parish in your town. This is her name. Do you know her? Could you find out for me if she really is a member there? Also, what is her family like?"

Example H: "Hey, big brother. I just met a guy who says he was in your high school class. Do you remember him? What was he like? What did you and your friends think of him back in high school?"

Example I: "Sis, can you stop by the coffee shop (park, gym, etc.) on Saturday afternoon? There's a young woman I want you to meet. I'd like you to start hanging out with us. I'd like to know what you think of her."

Helping by Focusing on Financial Planning

Financial stability is one of the foundations of a peaceful, happy marriage. Financial instability, on the other hand, is a major factor leading to divorce. Young adults generally do not realize how a good cash flow is necessary to maintaining a good marriage. That is why parents need to educate them.

Parents need to start discussions about the financial cost of marriage and raising a family because young people rarely will. The purpose of such discussions is to prepare a young adult for future financial responsibilities. There are many ways to start the conversations.

- A mother may say to her daughter, "Honey, did you ever wonder how much money it took to raise you and your brother? To pay for this house, the cars, the phones, our food, and everything else?"

- A father can say to his son, "Patrick, you say you want to get engaged? How long do you think it will take you to save up for a ring?" (Have the same talk about buying a car, saving up for car insurance, renting an apartment, going on a honeymoon, etc.)

- Or, "Patrick, have you ever wondered how much money you need to make a year to raise a family?"

- Or, "Honey, you said you would like to have children and stay home to raise them yourself. How will you have the money to do that? Where will the money come from?"

Conduct these conversations in a relaxed, low-key environment. One good time is when the parent and child are driving some distance in the car. Going for a hike or a recreational walk is another frequent setting. Eating out as a family allows a parent to guide a discussion about finances so all of the children hear and benefit from it. (From personal experience, I recommend treating the kids to a favorite food; mine really listened best when eating ice cream.)

At the very least, as the parent feels it is appropriate for the child's age and understanding, a parent should try to share and discuss the following financial information:

- The cost of running the household where the child was raised, including the salary of each working parent. Besides monthly costs, include the amounts paid for property, income and excise taxes, home, car and health insurances, and retirement plans. If the family took vacations, include a round figure of how much each vacation cost. Daycare expenses should be noted. If the children went to private schools or summer camp, include those figures as well. Allow for inflation.

- The various ways of saving and investing money, including savings accounts, bonds, stocks, hedge funds, etc. If you the parent need more information, consult a good accountant or financial planner and take your children with you so you can all benefit from the consultation.

- The amount of money that persons of different occupations make.

Consider two hypothetical situations:

Example A: Person A works for your town in a labor or clerical job for $40,000 per year. They have to work forty hours a week, with extra money for overtime. With that, A gets health insurance, a retirement plan, and four weeks of vacation a year. If A gets hurt on the job, there are good disability benefits. A's job is relatively secure, but A's salary will not increase much over A's lifetime.

Example B. Person B works a professional job at the local hospital and makes about $100,000 a year, getting similar benefits as Person A. However, B only gets two weeks of vacation a year and may have to work 50 or more hours a week with no extra pay for overtime. B's salary may increase if she advances in her profession, but she could also lose her job overnight.

Your goal as a parent is to get your children to think about finances and the importance of money. By doing so, you are educating your children about one of the important foundations of a stable marriage. Later on, your children will decide how important money is to them. They will also decide if money is important enough to influence their choice of a career or whom they marry.

Then, relax. Whatever will be, will be. As the parent, you have done your job. You passed onto your children your financial wisdom and knowledge. Later on in life, your children cannot blame you for not having educated them about money.

Helping by Giving Specific Feedback

"Doctor O'Hara, do you think it's a good idea to tell my daughter that I know her boyfriend is dealing drugs? I don't think she has any idea," one father asked me during a session.

When parents ask whether to tell their son or daughter something like this, I generally encourage the venture, especially if the parent appears to be acting in the best interest of the child.

Friends may also notice things. Both parents and friends need to offer feedback if they become aware of a boyfriend's or girlfriend's serious negative characteristics. Such feedback may be upsetting at first, but in the long run, the single person usually appreciates the well-intentioned effort.

If you are thinking of delivering negative information, I recommend the following four steps as a guideline:

First, check out the information. Make sure the information is based on fact, not on gossip or slander.

Second, evaluate the information. Is this information important for your single person to know? Would you yourself want to know this information if it were about your girlfriend or boyfriend? If the answer is yes, proceed with a conversation.

Third, be very kind. Your talk should be private and face-to-face if possible. This way your single person can see your concern and ask questions more easily. Try to follow this format:

- Say something positive and preparatory first. "We have been friends for a long time…" Or "As your father/mother, I love you very much, so I thought you should know what I found out."

- Give the information in a kind, calm manner. Remember that you are talking to someone you love.

- Give the information briefly and simply. "We have been friends for a long time. Because I care for you, I need to tell you some information about your boyfriend.

- Be ready to discuss how you obtained the information and whether your sources are credible.

- Express your regret about having to bring such news because you only want to see him or her happy.

- If your single wants to keep the information confidential, agree to it. If your single does not want to discuss your information, change the topic and talk about something else. You have done your duty as a good parent or friend.

Fourth, if in spite of your best efforts the information is poorly received, your single person may become angry and stop talking to you. Sensitive communication carries this risk. If there is an upset, in most cases it is soon mended.

Parents and friends have more to lose by withholding information than they do by raising it. Let's say you have some negative information but decide to say nothing. Consider what may happen later on. If the person finds out that you withheld important information, even though it happened long ago, they might feel that you could have prevented their bad marriage and/or consequent divorce if you had only warned them. Then the person blames you for having said nothing when your information might have prevented their losing the house in the divorce (or other hard times). Do you want to be in that position? That is where you might end up if you keep your silence now.

Helping by Acting as Same-Gender Evaluators

Teenagers and young adults should talk to their family members about who they are meeting and dating. The dates should meet family members as soon as possible. The meetings can be informal and on neutral ground. (Never invite someone you just met into your car, apartment, or family home.) For example, a father can meet his daughter's new boyfriend at lunch. A new girlfriend can be invited to meet a young man's sisters on a night out. Remember two important points:

• Men are better judges of men than women are

• Women are better judges of women than men are

If you are a single woman and you have smart male relatives willing to meet the men you date, consider yourself blessed. Older men can be especially helpful. They pick up on cues that women rarely notice and will make quiet inquiries about your young man, especially if you ask them to do so. All you need to do is ask.

If you are a single man and have wise female family members willing to meet the women you date, you too are blessed. Older females recognize such qualities as exhibitionism, hypomania, eating disorders, self-centeredness, or shifting moods. Young women with such traits initially appear to be fascinating, exciting, and independent creatures so that it is easy for a young man to misinterpret these traits, especially if the woman is pretty and the man is already infatuated. In such situations, the advice of female relatives can save a man from making a big mistake.

On the other hand, the advice of family members may be very positive. Upon getting to know the person you are dating, male or female family members may approve of your choice. Wouldn't that feel great?

What if the person you are dating is reluctant to meet your family members or friends? What if they attend a family gathering, but they act distant and do not join in conversations? In that case, I suggest you stop dating them. If a person is disrespectful to your loved ones, they are also being disrespectful to you. It is unlikely that you will be happy being married to them.

For Singles: Consult Family Members and Friends

Why are trusted family members and friends good resources and why should you, a single person, ask for their opinion about whom you are dating? You should because:

- Older family members have lived longer than you and have lots of experience in evaluating people. Their opinions can be helpful to you whether you are a younger or older single person, never married or divorced. Family and friends love you and want to see you happy. They have your best interests at heart and would never intentionally mislead you. Quite the opposite, they watch your back for you.

- Out of fear of offending you, they may withhold their opinion of your date unless you ask for it. Since their opinion is likely valuable to you, you would be missing valuable information important in making your choice.

- The more feedback and information you have, the better the decision you make. Even if you eventually disregard their information, you had the chance to weigh it in your decision-making.

- If their feedback about your date were positive, wouldn't you would want to know that?

Asking for feedback is not the same as having someone make a decision for you. It does not take anything away from your choice of whom to date or to marry. Asking for feedback means you are smart and grown up enough to listen. Asking for feedback means you recognize trusted family and friends as important resources.

It is up to you to be disciplined enough to ask for the type of help you need. In the next chapter I discuss the importance of being disciplined in the process of marrying well.

9

The Importance of Being Self-Disciplined

Discipline breeds success.

William G. O'Hara

I wrote this book because I believe most people can make a good marriage. I would like to see more and more people happily married. I would like to see fewer people get divorced. If you can discipline your mind and actions, a good marriage is yours for the making. Much of what I suggest in this book requires self-discipline.

The next time you think of the people you know, think in terms of self-discipline. Who is self-disciplined and who is not? You'll find that the ones who are focused and disciplined are more accomplished (better grades, jobs, bank accounts, etc.) and have a cleaner track record (no DUIs, bankruptcies, court records, etc.) than the people who are not. Self-discipline is also crucial in your selecting a suitable spouse.

Characteristics of Self-disciplined People

Self-disciplined people are able to manage their thoughts so that they reject myths. Similarly, they are able to identify meaningful and relevant acceptance and rejection criteria. Self-disciplined people can proceed to the next steps involved in marrying well. They discipline their social interactions, employ safeguards, talk in a purposeful manner, and restrain their emotions until they know they can trust someone.

Self-disciplined people take into consideration feedback from family and friends. Self-disciplined people make self-improvements and other changes in their lives as needed.

You already met Mark (see chapter seven) and know his story. The reason Mark was able to make a good marriage was because he worked hard and exercised self-discipline. It was not easy for him to stop drinking and take all the necessary mental steps to move forward. The reason Mark accomplished what he wanted to do was because he kept a sharp mental focus on his goal and stayed disciplined.

Characteristics of People who Lack Self-Discipline

Compared with self-disciplined people, undisciplined people are less successful in marrying well.

Undisciplined people may understand the difference between myths and reality but continue to believe in myths. Emotionally undisciplined people like Karen (in chapter one) allow physical attraction and emotion (instead of solid criteria) to lead them into poor marital choices.

Undisciplined people make up screening criteria just as well as disciplined people. However, because they get distracted and become emotional, they do not follow through. When the time comes, they forget to apply their criteria to their conversations and decisions. That is why they make poor decisions.

Part Two

From reading part one, you know that I like my work. The psychological problems that people share make me think, which I enjoy. The treatment of these problems allows for creativity and the chance to assist others, which I find rewarding.

Every person who comes through my office door is important to me. We get to work; we define the problems, set treatment goals, and stay focused on the job at hand. My style is interactive; I am supportive, reflective, and confrontational as, in my opinion, the situation requires. I listen hard to everything a client says and look for nonverbal behaviors.

People sometimes ask me what the purpose of psychotherapy is. I tell them that the purpose of my psychotherapy work is to assist my clients to become self-counseling so that they no longer need therapy.

Part Two contains stories* of real psychotherapy clients. I selected these from hundreds that I could have written about. I describe how some of these clients moved forward and succeeded in marrying well. Some of the clients had never been married before; others were already divorced when they came to therapy and wanted to marry better the next time. Names and identifying information have been changed, although the situations, presenting problems, and progress in therapy are genuine.

A word of caution to my readers: Not every idea you read about works for everybody, because everyone and every situation is different. However, you are welcome to use any of the ideas and suggestions if you think them helpful to you.

A cautionary word about psychotherapy is also appropriate. In Part Two, I selected the stories of people who made forward movement in their lives. These clients thought hard about what they wanted in a spouse, selected and applied their screening criteria, and sometimes improved their lives for the better. They made smart choices, which in most cases led to finding good marriage partners.

Ideally, the therapy process helps people correct past mistakes and overcome hardships. In therapy people have a chance to change their thinking and behavior so they make better choices in the future. However, therapy is not always a process of forward movement. Rather, therapy can have progressions and regressions. It is also used to maintain emotional stability or to prevent a condition from becoming worse.

* I am using the word *stories* to communicate to a lay readership interested in understanding the process of how to marry well. In no sense are these case studies as understood in the clinical, psychological sense where the studies are presented to peers for analysis and feedback.

10

More Trouble with Mythical Thinking

Who you marry determines your life.

Marilyn Moussa

In chapter one I discussed six harmful myths people believe about love and marriage. Belief in these myths can lead to heartaches and failed relationships, but people continue to believe them because they:

- Are too inexperienced to know any better

- Do not have confidence in themselves or think poorly of themselves

- Do not want to change their thinking and behaviors

- Like simple ideas and mistakenly believe that life too is simple

- Have not learned to think for themselves

Tom believed in a myth because he was too inexperienced to know any better. Read on to see how he changed his thinking.

Tom Loves Two Women at Once—Debunking Myth #4

Tom plopped himself into my armchair and lowered his head. When he looked up, I saw the tension in his face continue into his arms and tightly clenched fists. He could hardly contain his emotions.

"I hate myself," he groaned. "I am a good for nothing two-timer."

It took some time to understand Tom's self-loathing. His story was that he loved one girl, got engaged to her, and then fell in love with someone else. He cheated even though he didn't plan on it. Something else added to his underlying pain. Tom's father was the type of man who cheated. Seeing the pain this caused his mother, Tom swore he would never do that. Yet, here he was, twenty-one years old and already a cheater. Tom told me he was broken and abnormal like his father. He came to therapy out of desperation. He wanted me to fix him. Therapy was his last hope.

Little by little, Tom gave me the details. He dated Danielle during their first two years of college. Then, during his junior year, he went to study abroad, but not before getting engaged and setting the wedding date for the day after graduation.

Once abroad, Tom spent little time with the other American students. He immersed himself in the local culture and mixed with the natives. Once, he was lost in the city and a pretty young woman named Anna started talking to him. She spoke good English and helped Tom with directions. She also asked to practice her English with him by explaining the historical significance of nearby landmarks.

Another time, Tom saw Anna at the university. Anna invited Tom to a cultural event and gave him a tour to some parts of the city that foreigners rarely visited. Tom found himself entertained and pleased that he was learning so much about a new country. He admired that Anna was fluent in several languages. He started to think of Anna as a friend. He mentioned Anna to Danielle back home.

"I wasn't hiding anything. Danielle seemed happy that I was getting the special tours, but she said I should pay Anna for her efforts so Anna would know that it was strictly business."

Tom thought that a good idea. He told Anna he would like to pay her for the time she spent giving him guided tours and explaining cultural events.

"Well, Doctor, Anna would take no payment," Tom explained. "She said she felt honored to teach me about her country. She also said that not everything should be counted in monetary terms. That felt like a dig at my being an American and financially better off. She implied that I had somehow insulted her. That totally confused me. I dropped the topic. I never did pay her."

Anna invited Tom on trips into the countryside. Tom realized he was isolating himself and that people were talking about him, but he continued spending time with her. One night there was dinner and dancing in a country restaurant. While dancing with Anna and gazing into her eyes, she confessed that she loved him. Tom realized he was in love with her as well. Before he knew it, he was in bed with Anna. That is how Tom came to be in love with two women at once.

"I don't even know where I went wrong," Tom continued. "I had no intention of being a two-timer. Now I see myself as bad a man as my father was. What is wrong with me? Can I change? Do you help people like me?"

"I am going to try, Tom. Let's start by getting to know you first." Tom nodded his consent. "What led you to set a wedding date with Danielle before you went overseas? You were twenty years old then. What made it feel right for you to get engaged?"

"What are you getting at, Doctor?" His voice was uncertain, a little hostile.

I noted the defensiveness. "What I mean is that you could have waited until after you came back from abroad."

"Oh, I thought of that. But I did not want to risk losing Danielle. I found the right woman, and I did not want her to get away. She is still the right one for me. She did nothing wrong; I am the one who screwed up."

Tom was young and insecure enough to believe in the myth that there was only one right girl in the world for him. That is why he asked Danielle to commit to him in marriage before he went overseas. That is why he got confused and depressed when he fell in love with Anna.

The more we talked, the more I realized that Tom's problem was youth and inexperience. His loving two women at once was not an inherited moral shortcoming as he feared. What he needed to do was get to know himself and women better. He needed time to mature. He needed time to get rid of the myth that there was only one right girl in the world for him.

"Tom, may I share some ideas with you?" I asked, hoping to debunk his mythical thinking. "I wonder if you would listen for a little while. What I see as the problem here is your belief that there is only one woman in the world for you. This is a problem because in reality there are several people who may be right for you. You've maybe met two of them so far, although you don't know Anna very well. There may be more in the future."

Tom looked even more confused, but he did not ask me to stop.

"You see, there are many nice women out there. The longer you live, the more of them you meet. There can be many 'right' women for you, even for marriage. There is not just one right one."

"Okay, so if that's the case, how do I stay faithful to one woman?" he asked. "How does any man do that? That's what I wanted to do, and I failed."

"A failure? Maybe. But how about looking at this as a learning experience instead?"

I had Tom's full attention now, so I kept talking. "You could call it a moral failure if you were a thirty-year-old man of the world. If you were, you would know more about people and how to hold yourself to firm marital boundaries. But you are only twenty-one and inexperienced with women. You appear to be a good person. You are attractive inside and outside. I expect that young women would want to get to know you, spend time with you, and commit to you. I do not believe that is a moral failure to get sidetracked the way you did. In my opinion, your mistake was caused by inexperience, not because you are a bad person."

"Do you really mean this?" Tom asked in amazement. "I expected something different. I thought you would read me the riot act for being a cheater." Somewhat later he asked, "So how do I become wiser with women and not hurt anyone?"

We focused on Tom realizing that a decision to commit to one person does not always overrule feelings of physical and emotional attraction to someone else. Such attractions come during a lifetime, so Tom needed to learn how to deal with them in a mature manner. He needed to learn how to set boundaries and keep business and personal situations separate.

We also talked about the human capacity to love, which you either have or do not have. People like Tom carry it inside themselves wherever they go. That is why people can find someone to love most everywhere they live. Tom also needed to realize that when he was lonely and away from loved ones, he was vulnerable to becoming emotionally involved.

After a few sessions, Tom said he understood how his emotions got carried away with Anna.

"How are you doing?" I asked him one day.

Tom thought it over for some time. "Right now, I think I need to be single. I need time to think things through. I have been thinking of Danielle. I no longer believe that there is only one right girl in the world for me, but Danielle does have all the qualities I am looking for. But she is hurting now, and we broke up."

"What about Anna?"

"I did love her once, but she is not right for me," Tom replied without hesitation. "The situation and circumstances were all wrong. Actually, someone pointed out that I was very stupid. I now see what you mean about my being inexperienced."

I waited.

Tom continued, "You see, I now believe that Anna fooled me. She knew about my commitment to Danielle. Still, after the night in the restaurant, she wanted to get engaged and come to live in my country. I was shocked. Now I realize that I did not really know her. Later someone from the transfer program said Anna had gotten serious with another foreign student the year before I came. He implied that her intention was to marry an American citizen and live in the States. But since she made it seem like she loved her own country, I never once thought she would want to leave it. Stupid me. I believed everything she said. Well, I did love her, and maybe she loved me a little too."

"This is how we all learn," I said. "We make mistakes. Then we use the mistakes to become better people."

Tom continued to learn about himself. He realized he had emotional needs that could override his well-thought-out decisions. For example, a woman like Anna perceived an emotional need of his (to get into the city and learn about the culture) and capitalized on it for her own private welfare and gain (to marry an American and live in the States). Tom learned that some but not all people do this to other people all the time. In the future, if Tom saw someone going out of their way for him, he would pause and ask himself, *Why is this person spending so much time and effort with me? What is in it for them?* By asking such questions, Tom could provide balance for his naturally trusting nature. By questioning other's people's motives, he would gain time to think and not leap into a relationship.

In therapy, Tom was able to piece together how Anna's needs and how his own immaturity and mythical thinking intersected and caused his cheating. He also learned about the importance of boundaries and how he needed to use them for his protection.

Tom already had screening criteria for the type of person he wanted to marry. Once he understood that everyone makes mistakes, he forgave himself and started to date. He practiced being assertive. He asked questions of the women he saw. He tried to understand what they wanted out of life, what their values were, and what his own reactions were to them. He also learned to not signal his emotional needs. Furthermore, he learned to avoid placing himself in compromising situations.

Therapy stopped when Tom moved away. He called a year later to say hello. He was dating someone and was focused on advancing at his job. Two years later, he called again. He was dating yet another person and traveling overseas.

The third and last time Tom called, we had a longer conversation. He said he saw things differently from when he had first come to therapy. He now saw people as complex beings with multiple needs. He also felt more settled, secure, and accomplished. He was able to maintain boundaries with female friends, colleagues, and employees. He told me that the situation was right and he was getting married.

When I asked him whether he could stay faithful to one woman even though he may be attracted to others, Tom responded with a confident, "You bet."

When I asked him who he was marrying, he said, "Danielle."

I smiled. I recalled the day I had met Tom and how worried he was about being broken and abnormal. He was nothing of the sort. He was just another nice, young person whose belief in a myth left him confused and unhappy.

II

Selecting Acceptance and Rejection Criteria

Discipline is remembering what you want.

David Campbell

To make a good marriage, your thinking has to be disciplined and guide your emotional involvement. You need to keep your eyes wide open and focus your thinking. The problem with many relationships is that people get involved based on mythical instead of realistic thinking.

There is great value in stepping back and taking the time to think about the attributes and characteristics of the person you would like to marry. Your thinking can be shaped into acceptance and rejection screening criteria. I want to describe how Carla and Meg shaped theirs.

Carla Decides to Stop
Drinking and Changes Her Whole Life

People are complex beings. The complexity has a bearing on how therapy moves along and how people learn to solve their issues. The more complex a person's problems are, the more discussions are likely to arise, so that therapy sometimes moves backward, sideways, and forward. The therapist needs to understand the interactions of all problems and work with all of them to assist the client in general forward movement.

I am including Carla's story to show how a person with several issues can make progress. I will discuss some (but not all, due to space limitations) of these issues. I will also describe how Carla opened her eyes and learned to protect her heart.

One rainy fall day, Carla stated that she was ready to change and that she needed my help. Her anxiety was visible to me, but it was the determination in her voice that I noticed the most. Without any preliminary talk, she got right to the point:

"Doctor, for four years, all my friends and I did for fun was to drink alcohol." Carla talked in a direct, clipped, scripted way. "Now I want to get away from it. I have plans for the future, and I won't be able to carry them out if I don't stop."

Looking straight at me, she asked, "Can you help me?"

She was a recent college graduate doing secretarial work in her uncle's office. As it so often happens when people abuse alcohol and other drugs, when Carla drank she made poor choices. She said and did stupid things and found herself in one unpleasant entanglement after another. She hated her behaviors and wanted to change. After four years of hard drinking every Thursday, Friday, and some Saturday nights, Carla wanted to stop.

Stopping can be hard enough, but for Carla it was only the first step, although the most important one. Later I learned that Carla wanted a lot more. She wanted to find new ways to social-

ize, to let go of some of her best friends (i.e. d
and learn how to have a relationship with a m

Since this is more than what most people
they come to therapy, I wondered if Carla w.
about how much change she could make. As time went on, how
ever, I found her receptive to suggestions, willing to try new
ideas and behaviors, and above all, determined to change. Carla
had a way of making things happen.

She was particularly embarrassed about her past with men. In
college, she drank and hooked up but never had a relationship.
Many classmates considered her promiscuous.

She wanted to move beyond that; she wanted a new life.
She was going to graduate school, and with it came a chance to
start over. A different Carla would be going to graduate school.
Through hard work in therapy she planned to stop drinking,
shed her reputation, and exchange her self-loathing for feelings
of self-worth.

She did some of it right away. She stopped drinking without
a problem. She worked extra hours. She started going to a gym.
However, she still did not like herself. She also could not talk to
any of her friends about what she was doing differently.

One of Carla's problems was that she could say what she
thought in my office but not outside of it. Her fear was that if
she were honest, her friends would reject her. Despite her fear,
she needed to tell people that she was turning her life around.
Fortunately, an opportunity soon arose to do this.

"Doctor, I am going to my college alumni weekend in a few
weeks," she said one day. "This is when my college friends will
see that I have changed my ways. I know they will be drinking,
and when they see that I don't drink, there will be questions. I
think they will pressure me to drink. They will think me a joke.
Worst of all, one of the guys I used to fool around with will be
there, looking for sex."

Carla liked to take notes as we talked. I smiled and put a fresh pad of notepaper in her reach. ,

"Carla, the alumni weekend is a golden opportunity for you," I said. "It does not have to be something to be afraid of. Let's look at this as a chance to put your gains to the test. How could you do that?"

In the next few therapy sessions, Carla focused on strategies to get through the weekend the way she wanted to. She wanted to be sober, in control, and ready with answers for people who might question her. Interestingly, most of the strategies came from Carla herself.

"First of all, just because it is my first time, I am going to limit my participation in the weekend to one overnight only," Carla told me.

"How might you do that?"

"I will drive down on Saturday at noon and go to the hockey game with my friends that afternoon."

"Do you expect that there will be drinking at that event?"

"The hockey game will be on campus. Technically alcohol is only consumed in a bar on campus. That's *technically*. What might really happen is that a few people will be drinking out of bottles in brown bags at the hockey game, but not that much. The real drinking will be later, out on the town."

"How will you handle being out on the town?"

"This is where I need help. I want to attend an alumni reception after the hockey game and then go out with my friends. I need strategies. I do not want to drink."

I said, "Why not just say the truth? Why not just tell your friends where you are going in life and how you see things now? The way you have been telling me, right here in therapy?"

Carla winced, hesitated, and then agreed. "Yeah, okay. I can start on it tonight, on the phone. I am going to let one of my friends know. I'll say I won't be drinking. I guess I'll find out if she really is my friend."

"When you talk to your friend, Carla, how about saying things the way you do here in the therapy room? Simply. Nicely. Say that your decision is for yourself, that you feel more comfortable not drinking. Stay calm and in control. If your friend starts to pressure you and you feel uncomfortable, you have every right to stop the conversation. Just say that you have to go, and get off the phone."

"I'll try that," Carla said in a tentative tone. "She will be shocked. And I will have an earful for you the next session."

When I saw her a week later, Carla's eyes were dancing with joy. Behind closed doors, she let it all out. In her excitement, she could not sit down. She walked around in my office, clasping her hands and smiling ear to ear. "My prayers have been answered."

"Doctor, here it is." Carla was still too excited to take her seat. "I made myself do it. I told one of my friends that I was making changes and not drinking anymore. And guess what? She said she was stopping too. Her reason is different, though."

"How do you mean?"

"Her name is Denise. Well, Denise has been feeling blue since we graduated from college. She went for a physical exam and told the doctor that she was depressed. Her doctor asked her how much she drank. Ha! I know Denise lied. You have no idea how bad we were in college. I am embarrassed about it now. Anyway, the doctor said she would prescribe Denise an antidepressant, but only if she cut way back on her drinking. She's restricted to two small glasses of wine a week."

"What did Denise say to that?"

"Oh, she hated the idea at first. But she likes her doctor, so she agreed. Then she worried about how to tell me. Can you imagine? Both of us worried about telling each other that we've stopping drinking at the same time? Who would've ever thought? We were such drinkers."

"So has Denise stopped?"

"Yes. And the doctor said she could only have two glasses of wine during all of alumni weekend. But Denise is thinking, heck, who wants just two glasses' worth? That is like nothing. She's not even going to bother with that. So she is stopping altogether."

"You seem so happy, Carla. This is an exciting development."

"But there's more." Carla was sitting down, but just barely, on the edge of her chair. "Denise and I hatched a strategy for the weekend. We agreed that neither of us would drink and we would stick together at the bars. We will order non-alcoholic and hold those drinks in our hands all night. We're going to do alumni weekend sober. When everyone finds this out, they won't believe it. I can't believe it myself!" Carla's voice was ecstatic.

"What I am happiest about is that I developed my own strategy with Denise." Carla continued, "You taught me to think like that, but I developed one on my own."

"You most certainly did, Carla. Good for you, and good for Denise! So it sounds like you have alumni weekend all figured out!"

"Doctor, there is one more thing," Carla said and winced in the way that was so familiar to me by now. "I will be seeing Thomas when we go to the bars. In college, Thomas and I would hang out. Both of us would get drunk and have sex. This weekend, I'll see him with my friends, and he'll be thinking we'll hook up. The bottom line is I seem to like Thomas, but I don't know him. We always just drank."

In my opinion, Thomas was probably in the past. The real issue was how Carla would relate to men in the future. The past she could learn from and leave behind. Her present and future interactions with men would define Carla's feelings of self-worth.

This was an issue Carla could work on in preparation for alumni weekend. Now that she was sober, what did she want from a relationship? What kind of a man she would accept? Not accept?

I suggested to Carla that she think about all of this before we discussed specific strategies as to how to handle Thomas. I suggested that she develop screening criteria, starting with the acceptance criteria first.

Carla agreed. With typical gusto, she threw herself into the task of formulating ten acceptance screening criteria. She went home, made her list, and faxed it to me before the next therapy session so that I could review her criteria prior to our meeting.

Having identified the kind of a man she was looking for, we were ready to discuss how she might interact with Thomas. I invited her to devise a plan.

This was not because I did not want to do it for her. I do it sometimes. In Carla's case, I thought she could make her own plan. I invited her to do it because the ultimate goal of therapy is to teach people to be self-counseling. Making plans to handle tough situations is a step toward self-counseling. I thought Carla could take this step.

I waited a little, looking at her. Some time passed. I finally said, "How about handling Thomas the way you approached Denise? You seemed to do that very well."

"Yes. Um. Thomas is a guy. That makes it different," Carla pointed out.

"There might still be a sexual attraction, but otherwise, everything is the same. You can override the sexual attraction. Why not just tell Thomas the truth? Why not just tell him where you are going in life and how you see things now? The way you told me. The way you told Denise."

"What if he does not believe me? What if he laughs at me?" Her voice was tense, and she winced.

"Then he is not treating you respectfully. Then he does not meet your criteria, does he? If he laughs at what you are honestly saying about yourself, then he does not respect your feelings, and you don't spend time with him. If he does that, you can just say, 'It's been nice talking to you' and walk away from him. Move on to talk to someone else."

"So that's okay to do?"

"Why would it not be? By walking away from him you emphasize that you are serious about what you said."

"What if he never talks to me again?"

"If he never talks to you again, it is his loss. It just means that he can't let go of the old pattern of drinking and hooking up. He looks at you as a hook-up partner, not as a person. So why would you care if he does not talk to you again?"

"Okay, I get it. That's right. For my personal life, I am interested only in those men who meet my criteria. So if Thomas laughs at me and doubts me, he is just wasting my time."

With a sigh, Carla went off to her weekend.

To her surprise and relief, she had a great time. She met and talked with a lot more people than she did while in college. She talked about her goals for the future. She was amazed when a few male alumni expressed an interest in having lunch with her. Thomas turned out to be a non-issue. He was drinking heavily. Carla found herself uninterested in talking to him. So she and Denise only said hello and socialized with other people.

Carla's success at alumni weekend allowed her to feel more comfortable with herself and men. She realized she had more fun being sober. She saw that she could interact in constructive, non-sexual ways and that nice men found her attractive and interesting. She could put the past behind her.

Since Carla was feeling so much better about herself, she realized that in the future she could choose among men. She was now in a good psychological position to develop rejection criteria. Using both her acceptance and rejection criteria, Carla would have a clear idea about the type of man she was looking for and also the type of man she would not spend time with.

Beautiful Meg Cannot Find a Man to Marry

Many years ago, a very attractive young woman named Meg came to see me. Little did I know then that I would be helping her develop acceptance and rejection screening criteria.

Naturally blonde, lovely in face and figure, Meg settled into my armchair and began to cry. The sobbing got deeper before she could speak, and I wondered if I was seeing the symptoms of a deep pathology.

"My life is in shambles, and I do not know why." Meg sobbed into a fistful of tissues.

"Please tell me what you mean."

"I mean that I am a loser. I wish I did not have to come here. Why am I the way I am? I hate myself!"

The words came forth like blood pulsating from a bad wound. I pushed the wastebasket to Meg so she could throw the wet tissues away. I settled back in my own chair and hunkered down for whatever I might hear. I wanted Meg to see from my body language that I would take time to listen to her.

Most clients like to present a well-organized story of their lives, but Meg was in no condition to do so. The first hint that Meg's thinking was usually well ordered came from her frustration that she could not organize her thoughts.

"I have rehearsed what I would say to you so many times, but I am so upset now I can't remember or say any of it," Meg said, but I could see that she was a little less agitated than before.

"Meg, anyplace you start is okay. Take your time."

"Okay. Here it is. I can't get anyone to marry me."

What? I remember thinking. The most attractive woman I had ever seen was having trouble getting married? What was going on here? Meg seemed to read my thoughts.

"I know that I am good-looking." She wiped her tears and blew her nose. "But I can't stand it.

"God made me pretty," Meg continued. "Trust me, my appearance is not a blessing. When I was a child, people commented on my looks. As a young woman, men hounded me for it. Nobody ever got to know the real me. I got scared. During my twenties I stopped socializing. I stayed at home because I hated to go places where people would look at me. When I started dating I saw that men just want to sleep with my body. I never know if they are interested in me as a person. Maybe I have just my body, but I am not a person. Is that possible? That is how I feel."

Meg's sobbing and agony lessened as she spoke. I was glad to see that. But I was puzzled. Meg sounded as though she were alone in life. Where were her parents, family, and friends? Where were the people who usually impact one's life growing up and teach you about people, life, and how to love yourself? We talked a little longer. Eventually I asked about Meg's family of origin.

Meg described her upbringing. Her alcoholic dad and two brothers were the dominant forces in the family. Her mother and Meg provided for their needs. There was not much family conversation. Her father made the decisions, one of which was that her brothers should go to college but Meg should not. The father paid for her brothers' education; Meg struggled to put herself through the local state college after her father's death. Meg was always passive in interacting with her father and brothers. When she started dating, she sought to please. When a relationship became physical, she would either stop dating or have sex if she thought the man might propose marriage. No one ever proposed. Now she trusted no man. Worse, she did not value herself.

Meg's presentation of herself as being alone was true. Her elderly mom was sick, her father was dead, her brothers were distant. What was also important was that Meg was telling me that she was an adult child of an alcoholic (ACOA). From the research in this area, I knew that Meg most likely 1) doubted her capacity to love and be loved, 2) had low self-esteem despite her achievements, 3) was confused about what was normal in relationships, 4) put taking care of other person's needs before taking care of her own needs and became a caretaker, and 5) depended on others' feelings to know her own.

As with Mark in chapter seven, Meg and I would have many conversations about how her upbringing contributed to how she felt as a person. Later we would discuss how it might have led to dysfunctional relationships with men. One important therapy goal was for Meg to understand what a functional, normal relationship was like.

In my experience, it is particularly difficult for ACOAs to change the ways they think and view people. For people like Mark and Meg, it is hard to relax with healthy non-ACOAs. ACOAs generally perceive non-ACOAs as too different from themselves—too happy, too self-confident, too carefree and even as cocky. This difference is real. Non-ACOAs were raised in child-oriented families in which children could express themselves relatively freely and felt supported and valued by their parents. That is why non-ACOAs tend to be more spontaneous and easygoing as adults. Because ACOAs do not understand these happier, carefree, and spontaneous presentations, they tend to distance themselves from non-ACOAs. Because of this difference, ACOAs isolate themselves and are left with the company of other ACOAs (or alcoholics), whose behaviors they are more familiar and therefore comfortable with. They instinctively feel an unspoken kinship with each other, although their lives are generally unhappy. This perceived kinship results in many

ACOAs marrying other ACOAs or alcoholics. That is one reason why the cycle of drinking continues, generation after generation.

Well, here was Meg. She wanted to be married, but she did not want her mother's marriage. Rather, she wanted a happy marriage to someone who valued her and for me to help her reach that goal.

"Meg, what might help here is to reorient your thinking. It sounds as though you have been looking for signs of whether or not men want you for yourself. This may be because you did not get that at home from your father and brothers, so you want that from someone you would marry." Meg nodded in agreement, so I continued in an encouraging tone, "Of course a man should want you for yourself. But instead of looking for signs as to whether a man wants you for yourself, how would you like to be thinking about what you want in a man?"

Meg looked puzzled. It seemed as though she was hearing this for the first time.

I continued, "Meg, let me paint a picture for you. This picture is an analogy of what I mean. I would like you to picture yourself as a beautiful flower. As such, many bees are attracted to you just for your looks. So picture the men to be like bees. One man or bee may be for keeps, but the rest are not. You, the flower, need to decide which you will accept. To know which man you will accept, you need to be certain in your mind as to what kind of a man you are looking for."

Meg said she had never looked at it that way. In the past, she always kept conversations light, on the surface. She assumed that men made the decisions, including what you talked about. However, since her past was a disaster, she would try any new approach that made sense.

It worked. Meg started thinking. We discussed what an ACOA was. Meg did a lot of reading about growing up in alcoholic households and how the atmosphere of the household affected the children growing up in them. It was painful for her. She said she identified with the role of caretaker, but that was the last thing she wanted in her marriage.

As Meg made her list of what she was looking for in a husband and the father of her children, she struggled with the assertive statements she needed to make. As many ACOAs, she didn't know what she could or couldn't say. She also didn't know exactly how she felt. Most of all, she was afraid of being judged for her directness and honest feelings. The first topic concerned religion.

"I really want a man of my own religion. But then I am discriminating against men of other faiths. Discrimination is wrong. So I am stuck. I don't want to do something wrong."

"But are you doing something wrong by stating a personal preference?" I countered. "Let's think this through. Let's look at the context. Certainly if you made public statements such as standing on a street corner with a sign that said, 'Buddhists go home,' you would be discriminating against a religion. But in this criteria-selection situation, the context is strictly personal. It is okay to have personal preferences when you look for a spouse."

Meg did not appear convinced, so I added another thought. "Meg, many people prefer to marry someone of their own religion. That is not considered discrimination. That is a personal preference they are entitled to."

This was a new idea for Meg. I could see that no one had ever discussed such topics with her. It took her time to get used to such discussions. Her next struggle was the issue of a man's educational level, professional standing, and income. She knew what she wanted. But she thought she would be mean if she said that she did not want men under a certain income or educational level.

At this point I realized that in the past Meg had dated just about anyone who asked her. She had little sense that her thinking and desires counted for anything in life.

How to communicate to Meg that her will and desires were important? I was desperately searching my thinking when an idea came to me.

"Meg, are you familiar with the Declaration of Independence?"

"Yes. But what does that have to do with me?"

"Everything!"

"I don't get it."

"What it has to do with you is that in the Declaration of Independence of the United States it states that every person has a right to the pursuit of happiness. That includes you too. It is okay to act in the pursuit of your own happiness. What you are doing by stating your acceptance criteria is not discrimination. You are acting in the pursuit of your happiness."

I saw Meg's eyes light up. The idea worked. If an official historical document such as the Declaration of Independence mentioned happiness, then it made it right for her. One simple statement penned by the founding fathers of our country allowed Meg to accept her feelings as her right. The struggle was over. Meg finished her list of acceptance and rejection screening criteria without further discomfort.

A short time later, Meg declared herself ready to meet men.

But where were the men to meet or not to meet her criteria? Meg refused to go to singles' dances, bars, and class reunions. Her acquaintances were married, raising children, and too busy to help. Internet services were out of the question. Meg was thirty-five years old and in a hurry.

After much discussion and soul-searching about spending the money, Meg hired a high-end dating service to introduce her to eligible men. She was able to inform the service of her requirements for a man without any self-questioning. She wanted to meet men of her own religion, non-smokers, light social drinkers who didn't use illegal drugs, and had a certain level of education and income.

For the next six months, Meg was busy. The first seven refer-rals from the dating service produced nice enough men, but no one to marry. Meg shared her reasons for rejecting each one. She sounded self-confident. She was acting like the flower who was looking for that one bee. As time passed, however, she started worrying that the right bee would not fly to her. Was she being too picky? I saw the old doubts and worries resurface.

Then things changed. The last referral was a quiet, pleas-ant, well-established doctor who met all of Meg's criteria. They got engaged after a year of dating. This is not a fairy tale, in case you think it too good to be true. It is the very real story of how a beautiful woman who could not find anyone to marry her found marital happiness at last. Meg found happiness because she developed and applied the screening criteria that best repre-sented what she wanted and needed in a husband.

12

Learning to Talk

Do not lie in a ditch and say, "God help me";
use the lawful tools He lent thee.

English Proverb

Sometimes the nicest of people have terrible conversation skills. Once they have their acceptance and rejection criteria lists ready, they need help figuring out how to talk to people. Therapy is one place to get this help.

Shy Pamela Struggles and Succeeds with LIFE Topics

How Pamela made it through my door for the first appointment I will never know. Head down, eyes on the floor, she scampered into my office and stopped in the middle. I saw that her face was red and contorted when she lifted her head. I wondered if she were ill and was going to be sick in my office.

"Do you have a towel?" were Pamela's first words to me.

"I'm sorry, I do not. Do you need one?"

"I don't want to sweat onto your armchair cushions."

"I have paper towels. Will that be okay?"

"Oh, yes."

I watched Pamela place about half a roll of paper towels on the cushions and settle herself in the armchair. She seemed a little more relaxed.

Pamela's case was unusual in that she was a very shy and reserved person. I wondered if she ever had the joy of a good conversation. Or maybe no one ever really listened to her. She reported that whenever she talked about herself she broke into a sweat and worried about the sweat coming through her clothing.

Pamela wanted therapy to change her so that she could be more social. She wanted to meet people, she wanted to marry, and she came to therapy to find out how to talk to people.

All went well enough in the first few sessions. Pamela was able to establish rapport, started smiling, and talked more openly and fluently. However, once she finished her acceptance and rejection criteria, she panicked.

"I am sweating through my underwear at the thought of talking to strangers! I can't do it! I will die."

I decided to point out the gains Pamela had already made in therapy.

"Pamela, did you die when you first came into my office?"

"Almost."

"But you didn't."

"No. What are you getting at?"

"Let me ask a follow-up question. Am I not basically a stranger to you?"

"Yes…no. What do you mean?"

"Here's the point. You did not die coming to therapy, and you did not die talking to me, a complete stranger. What you did was a great job of overcoming your fears."

"Really?"

"You have done well talking in therapy, Pamela. You are articulate, well-spoken even."

"Really?"

"Yes. And I am a stranger to you. We have only known each other for a total of six hours, so I am basically a stranger, right?"

"I see. So maybe I can talk to strangers."

"That is what it looks like to me. It is only the fear in your head that is in your way. If you could come in to talk to me, you can talk to other people as well. So you sweat a little. So what? A lot of people sweat a little. You'll take a shower later. By the time you talk to the twentieth person, you will be much more relaxed."

"Twenty people! Your saying that makes me sweat all over again."

"With practice you might find that you are a good conversationalist."

"You don't know of any shortcut, do you, Doctor?"

"I wish I did. I would have patented it and become rich," I said, and Pamela laughed and relaxed a little, as I hoped she would.

"Instead of a shortcut, I have a little mental technique that might help you. I call it LIFE."

The mnemonic device LIFE (introduced in chapter three) is useful in starting and keeping conversations going. Even in a frightened condition, I thought Pamela would remember the word LIFE and what each of the letters stood for so that she could carry her share of a conversation. Each letter stands for a topic that she can ask another person about:

L is for livelihood; it is how a person makes his or her living

I stands for inspiration, such as the kinds of things that motivate a person

F is for family and friends

E is for entertainment, such as what a person likes to do in his or her spare time.

"I like it. It makes sense. It is my life that I am trying to turn around with LIFE!" Pamela concluded after thinking it over. "Only can I talk to a stranger who is a woman first? The idea of talking to men makes me nervous."

"Certainly," I said. "How about that nice woman in your aerobics class that you mentioned once? You could ask an E question to start with."

Pamela did not need help figuring out what to talk about. During the next visit, she happily reported that she had had a great conversation with her aerobics classmate. She started with E questions. The conversation quickly moved to L and I topics.

"Also, we work in the same part of town, so we are getting together for lunch next week. We are going to talk some more," Pamela explained. "She continued, "I know it won't be so good with everybody I meet. But now I feel I have a chance. Maybe I can try talking to a man. I'd like to work on how to do that."

Pamela committed to fine-tuning her conversation skills. In preparing to talk to men, we role-played, where I acted the role of different men. The role-playing process helped desensitize Pamela to the responses that men might make to her. It also helped her identify situations when she wanted to keep a conversation going or when she wanted to stop one. When she seemed ready, I had an important piece of advice for her: "Pamela, the important thing to remember is to not let it upset you if someone does not want to talk with you. Do not take it personally. Okay?"

"Why not? If he was just rude to me."

"If the man did not respond to you or if he was rude to you, it is his issue, not yours."

"I don't get it. What do you mean?"

"Well, maybe he is shy. Remember how shy you were?" I asked. "There could be other reasons for him not being talkative. He might have something on his mind, such as a problem. Or he does not know how to answer your question. He might not be talking for reasons of his own, nothing to do with you."

"I see. I'll try to remember that."

"If that happens, just move on. Or if someone is rude to you in another way, again, move on. Talk to someone else. Keep your focus on your LIFE and criteria topics. The right man will like you well enough as you are."

Pamela slowly relaxed and became more social. She stopped sitting on paper towels in my office. She had lunch dates with men and women. The months passed. Pamela held her head up and smiled most of the time.

A few years after she stopped coming to therapy, Pamela left a message on my confidential voicemail. Her voice was happy, confident. She said that she found a nice man and was engaged to be married.

13

THE USE AND MISUSE OF COMMON SENSE

Common sense ain't common.

Will Rogers,
American humorist

It is great to be in love, isn't it? Well, yes and no. The good part is the feeling of it. The bad part is that once you are in love, it is easy to fool yourself.

Being in love puts your emotions in charge of you. Your emotions try to hijack your thinking. For example, if a person does not meet your criteria, your hijacked brain gets busy explaining away the faults of the person. That is the way that being in love can keep you in a relationship when you should be running the other way.

It sometimes falls to me to point out the bad part of being in love. Doing this does not make me popular with clients, but sometimes it is what I have to do in my job as their therapist.

When I see that a client is not thinking clearly, I ask that they hear me out. After that, the client decides what he wants to do.

Sometimes the client will not listen. Stan was already in love when I tried to talk to him.

Stan Shows no Common Sense: He Disregards His Own Rejection Criteria

Stan was late for the therapy session. His lateness was due to his having to drive his girlfriend somewhere because she was arrested for driving drunk and her license was revoked. I recalled Stan's rejection criteria. In it he clearly stated that if a girl had a DUI, he was going to reject her.

"Yes, Doc, I did have no DUIs as one of my rejection criteria. I did say that."

"Well, this girl you really like just got a DUI. What do you think?"

"Nothing. It's not a problem, because I really believe that what Stephanie says is what really happened."

I try it again. "Stan, you have not known Stephanie for very long, have you? How come you are sure you can believe what she says?"

"Doc, this is what you don't understand. It must be because you are older and you forgot what it is like to love."

"Stan, of course I remember, but—"

There was no stopping Stan. He wasn't going to listen. He talked on. "It's true that we've only dated for a few weeks, but honest to God, we are like soul mates. I believe her totally. Stephanie said that her former boyfriend, who is a police officer, was mad that she broke off their engagement last month, so he had a fellow officer stop her after Stephanie had only one drink at the bar and was on the way home. The officer said Stephanie was driving erratically, whatever that means. But she was arrested when she would not blow the Breathalyzer, and the judge, who always sides with the cops, said she had to go for alcohol-abuse counseling. She has the DUI on her record, but it's all a mistake. So I don't think my rejection criteria of no DUI stipulation applies to Stephanie. Not in this case. She is an exception."

I try one more time. "Stan, I am not saying anything against Stephanie herself. I respect that you chose her to be your girlfriend. What I am saying is that for your own welfare, give this matter more thought. Try to find out if drinking could be an issue for Stephanie. There are many ways to do that."

"I won't do that. I believe her. We love each other."

Have you ever seen a situation like this? I have, too many times. Gullible, inexperienced Stan quickly fell in love with Stephanie. He made the mistake of quickly getting emotionally involved, and his emotions overrode his carefully thought out rejection criteria. What happened was that Stan drove his girlfriend around until she got her license back. Then the relationship failed because Stephanie wanted out. Stan was devastated. Looking back on it, Stan realized that he had been too hasty in getting involved with her. Next time around, he was going to honor his screening criteria.

Both men and women tend to jump into relationships when the chemical attraction of love is overwhelming. The feeling of love rules all reasoning for a while, after which the relationship often fails because chemistry and love alone cannot sustain it. Andrew's case is another example.

Andrew Learns From the Past

Andrew called my office and asked to be seen as soon as possible. The urgency in his voice was palpable. It just so happened that I had a cancellation and he could make that time. I found him on the edge of his seat in the waiting room. He took care of the preliminary paperwork in record time.

Andrew was a stylish, pleasant-looking, forty-year-old father of two young children. His smile appeared forced. He said he had many problems. His most immediate concern was that he had no time to relax. This was partly due to his visitation arrangement. His two children were by different mothers, and Andrew was struggling with his visitation schedule, which allowed him no free weekends for relaxation.

Then he had a relationship issue as well. "My girlfriend has just about had it with me. She's upset that I have no time for partying."

Partying at age forty? Of course, everyone's different, but it seemed like a topic worth exploring. This man was yearning for time to relax, and his girlfriend wanted him to party?

"Tell me about your girlfriend, Andrew," I said. "What is she like?"

"Oh, she is pretty and very social. I love going out with her. Everyone looks at her and then at me. I know they are thinking that I am a lucky guy." Andrew smiled for the first time. "I love that feeling. Especially when I take her to work-related socials. I know that the other men envy me."

"But, Doc, there is another side of me." Andrew tensed up a little, and I perceived that what he was about to say was very important to him. "I am not just about socializing. I want other things, but I don't have them. I worry that there is something wrong with me."

"What might be wrong with you?"

"I just have this feeling that I am doing something wrong with women. I think this when I compare my life to the lives of other men. Some men I know have been married only once. They have just the one wife and kids. Their lives are simple. They have money in their pockets. They relax and nap on the weekends.

They can go away on a golf weekend while the wife watches the kids. Why is that not my life too? Why is it as messed up as it is? It's got to be something wrong with me."

"These men live better than I do," Andrew continued. "They are not paying an insane amount of child support, and they have more free time than I do as a single man. I see them laughing. When have I laughed lately? Also, I bet they get lucky more often than I do."

"Andrew, you sound unhappy with your life. Let me ask another question: What do you think you are doing wrong with women?"

"Doc, I wish I could put my finger on it."

"What were your wives like? Maybe it would help if you described them to me."

"Just like my girlfriend. Very pretty, social, liked to go out. I guess I have this need to have pretty women. It makes me feel good to be with them. But the marriages haven't worked, it's a mess with the kids, and I am so unhappy."

So what did Andrew want? How could I assist him? "Andrew, what do you think would make you happy? I mean, right as you are sitting here, what do you wish for? Put it into words for me, please."

"I would like a marriage that works. I want to relax. I don't want to party. And because my girlfriend is just like my two ex-wives, I get worried."

Andrew was closing in on the important problem in his life, that he yet again had chosen the wrong kind of woman in dating his girlfriend. But to make the point more powerful, he needed to come to that conclusion himself. He needed to elaborate on how his girlfriend was similar to his wives. To focus his thinking, I asked, "How is your girlfriend similar to your ex-wives?"

"She is beautiful, like I said. She spends time on looking nice. My exes were partiers too. They drank a little too much; that's why they were fun at parties. But once I married them and we were at home, they weren't fun at all. They got nasty. Come to think of it, that's why I divorced them. You know what? My girlfriend is exactly like them. What am I doing?"

This insight was a turning point in Andrew's therapy. He now understood that the women he instinctively liked were stimulus-seekers who had to go out and party. They dressed, acted, and thought like teenagers. While Andrew had found that exciting in the past, he was realizing that it did not work to be married to them.

Andrew also needed to realize that his strong chemical attraction to a female is actually a counter-indication to his later happiness with her. In the future, he might look for a different type of woman and stay away from the ones he was immediately attracted to. His most immediate concern, however, was to sort out his current relationship. What did he want to do with it?

"Andrew, you understand the pattern you have gotten into with women. You seem saddened by it. Now, tell me, does your girlfriend want to get married?"

"She's hinted at it, and she's not being intimate with me now. Maybe she's mad that I don't have that ring. But I'm just not sure because I have been very wrong before. But she doesn't care. "

"So you feel forced into getting engaged?"

"Yeah. Just like the first two times. Exact same scenario." Andrew sat back in his armchair, and I saw his shoulders relax. It seemed like he was putting it all together. "That is just what it is. What do you docs call it? Déjà vu?"

"Indeed. Andrew, if you don't want to get engaged, why do it? If you need time to think things over, what is keeping you from taking that time?"

"Nothing, really. I guess I'll just lose a hot girlfriend. She'll move out of my house. I'll be single. But I'd rather do that than go through another divorce."

It was quiet for a while.

"Well, thank you, Doc. Do you have any suggestions? Because I clearly need a different approach to women."

"Well, I just may have something for you. It's about learning to not confuse the style of a person with the substance of the person." I saw the interest in Andrew's eyes, so I continued, "Would you like to talk about it?"

"That is just what I want. I want things to think about. I have to change how I do things."

I asked Andrew to imagine a room full of books, all of them different. Some have nice, attractive covers with nothing worthwhile to read inside them, others have attractive covers with interesting contents, still others have unattractive covers with interesting reading in them, and so forth. (A fuller description of this analogy can be found in chapter three.) The point is that just as you can't tell if there is anything useful inside a book by looking at its cover, so you cannot tell what a person is really like by her style or appearance. You can only tell what a person is really like by taking the time to look beneath her style and read her thoroughly.

Andrew got it. In the future, he would move beyond his chemical attraction to a woman. He promised himself that he would take his time getting to know what a woman was like, just as he would take the time to read a book to see if he liked what was inside it.

Andrew next made a list of screening criteria. These helped him to remember what he wanted to find out about women. Finally, for his own protection, he decided to avoid partying females.

"I never understood any of this before. I never talked to anyone about women like I have in here," Andrew reflected. "I always thought that a woman had to be hot, like in the magazines. I also wanted other guys to be envious of me. But what's there to be envious of? Two child support payments and no decent wife? I would be much happier with a wife I could love, respect, and relax with. I wish I had thought of all of this years ago."

When it came time to say good-bye, Andrew said, "Doc, thanks for your help. You turned my life around."

"Andrew, I did no such thing." I smiled back. "All I did was talk with you. It is you who will make it happen. You will turn your own life around, based on what you decided in here."

"But if I hadn't talked with you…yes, well. I have to carry on now. I will."

"Let me know if you need to talk again," I said. "My door is open to you."

Then Andrew left. When I next heard from him, his voice sounded relaxed, contented. He was dating a medical doctor. He said they had good conversations over dinner and that he understood the difference between style and substance now.

14

Is It a Lie or Is It Not a Lie?

Everybody lies.

> Dr. Gregory House, M.D.,
> from the TV Show *House*

When people meet, it is natural for them to want to make a good first impression. Unfortunately, some people go beyond the boundaries of a good impression and distort reality so much that they create a fake presentation of themselves.

Verification of information is your main safeguard against liars of all types. If you want a relationship based on the truth, it is up to you to check out what the truth is. The following case segments illustrate how people may lie and also how you can verify information.

Stephanie Checks Out What the Plumber Said

My client Stephanie was looking for a nice man. One day she told me she had met someone who was a plumber who had his own business. From the smile on her face, I gathered that Stephanie already liked him.

Naturally, doing my job, I suggested that she check out if he really was a plumber.

Just as naturally, Stephanie got upset (like many others have before her).

"Doctor O'Hara, I feel that I would be violating his privacy. Besides, I believe what he says."

"I appreciate your feeling that way, Stephanie, but you would not be violating his privacy. You would just be looking up public domain information. Millions of people—anybody with online access—can look to see if this nice man truly is a licensed plumber. You just log onto the board of registry run by the state and search the list of licensed plumbers. Then you can search your geographic area for him and his business."

After awhile, Stephanie seemed more at ease with the idea. But, being a very honest person, she had another question. "Well, then, do I tell him that I checked to see if he really was a licensed plumber?"

"That is up to you, Stephanie. You can tell him or not tell him."

"What if I tell him what I did and he doesn't like it?"

"That would tell a lot about him, wouldn't it?"

Stephanie looked puzzled. "What do you mean? What would it tell?"

"Perhaps he would be thinking that he does not want a woman who thinks for herself. Maybe he wants a more gullible, less bright person. Someone who wouldn't think to double-check on things."

Stephanie sat up straight. I saw her eyes harden a little. "So if he gets mad at me for checking out his licensure, I probably would not want him."

"Then again, Stephanie, he might like it that you had the initiative and resourcefulness to check him out. He might like you all the better for it. It depends on what he is like as a person."

"I get it." She smiled and relaxed. "This is how I find out what he is made of."

She was right. No one should automatically trust another person, especially when marriage is at stake. By checking out this information, Stephanie is choosing to protect herself emotionally (since she already liked the man) and give her plumber a chance to earn her trust.

Her trust would be earned if she verified that the plumber told her the truth about himself. Ideally this would happen not just once but repeatedly. Then it would be safer for Stephanie to trust him because she would have some assurance that he was an honest person.

As it happened, the man was a real, licensed plumber with a good business. This fact encouraged Stephanie to share with him that she had gone online to check him out. She was afraid that he would get mad, but instead of getting upset he offered her a part-time job in his office. As their relationship developed, Stephanie stopped coming to therapy because she no longer needed it.

Justin Verifies Information and Escapes Getting Deeper

Unlike Stephanie, Justin had no reservations about checking out any type of information. He told me of an incident with a woman who got mad that he checked her out.

"I was told by this woman I met that she owned a certain piece of property. She seemed very believable, but I thought I would like to see for myself. I happened to be at the Town Hall of the town she said she owned property in. The clerk was very helpful; she said that anyone could use the book of property listings. So I spent some time looking at who owns what property, property values, tax rates, and so forth."

"Yes, this is public information," I said. "What did you find?"

"Nothing. The woman owns no property in that town. The property that she was talking about is in the name of her brother and the brother's wife."

"What did you do with this information?"

"I decided to be honest about what I did, to see how she would take it. I figured you don't really know someone until you stress them a little. When people are stressed they are more likely to show themselves for who they are. So I told her what I did and asked her how she came to say that the property was hers. Well, she got mad and accused me of spying on her."

"How did you handle that?"

"Well, I just said to her, 'Hey, I can check on anything I want to check on.' I said it twice, actually. And then she started to explain that the property really should have belonged to her, but her brother cheated her out of it. She said she is going to court to get it back and she would succeed because she has the best attorney in town. So she was implying that she did not lie to me, not really."

"What do you think about that?"

"I think it is probably just another lie. She said the second lie to try to make herself look better for having told the first lie. I really don't care; I saw her first reaction. It was hostile. The second reaction was probably to save face, to put herself in a better light. In her mind, she is trying to justify that she had reason to say that she owned the property. Well, she can fool herself if she wants to, but she can't fool me."

"Justin, what do you think the chances are that she is right and that the courts will restore the property to her?"

"Who knows? The main thing is, I am no longer interested in her."

Compared to Stephanie, Justin was eager to verify information. (He actually could have done the checking from his home computer or portable device by logging onto the town's Web site and searching the property listings.)

Noteworthy in Justin's approach is that he immediately confronted the woman to see how she would handle his realizing that she had told what appeared to be a lie. (Confrontation is one way to find out what a person is like.) Now, had the woman been honest and smart enough to say, "Hey, I'm sorry I lied, but here is my reason..." Justin might have accepted the apology. But that did not happen. The woman got defensive instead. The sequence of her angry reaction, her statement that Justin had no right to check out the information, and then saying what seemed to be another lie provided Justin with enough negative information about her. He decided he was not going to waste his time talking with her because she clearly did not meet his screening criteria.

Richard Figures Out
Why Jackie Says One Thing and Does Another

Sometimes people lie by saying one thing and doing the exact opposite.

Twenty-two-year-old Richard became ill while vacationing abroad. When he arrived home, he had to be hospitalized. His condition deteriorated. He left his job as a mechanic, moved into his parents' house, and spent most of the time in bed. His recuperation took several months. Jackie, his girlfriend of three years, was generally patient and supportive. But once Richard was better and could go places with her, she declared that she wanted to take a break from the relationship.

Richard got upset and called me for an appointment.

"I really did not see this coming," he said through his tears. "She was with me throughout my illness. I am so grateful to her. I thought we had a great thing going."

"You wonder at her behavior and her words being contradictory. How about you ask her what it all means?"

At the next session, Richard had more information. "I told Jackie I was totally confused that she acted like she loved me when I was sick and now when I am better and can love her better she says she wants a break. What's her reason? It is because she can't forget that I was abusive to her three years ago."

"Oh? How were you abusive, Richard?"

"By taking her for granted. A few years ago I was in Philadelphia working on cars for a few months. Jackie would call and say she was worried about what I was doing, and I would just say, 'Can't talk to you now; I'm busy,' and just not pay attention to her feelings. I would call her at night, though, when I was finished working. But she means that I didn't talk to her when she needed me. That's how I was abusive to her."

"What do you think about this?"

"I am confused. Maybe I was mean to her, but that was three years ago when we were both nineteen years old. I've tried to be a good boyfriend since then. Why is she bringing up all of this stuff now? And do you know what she is doing? She's telling me that she wants me to hang out with her once a week, because she does not want to lose me. I love that. But then, in the next breath, she tells me that she and her girlfriends are going to a frat party on Saturday night."

Two weeks later, things were worse. Jackie was now spending the night at the fraternity house because she was too drunk to drive herself home. Richard was beside himself.

"I just don't get it. She invited me to go shopping with her on Saturday. We went to the mall, and I bought her dinner. Then she leaves me and goes to this foam party at the frat house and spends the night. She said she spent the night on a couch, but how do I know that she wasn't in someone's bed?"

What Jackie could not tell Richard, she conveyed with her actions. When Richard objected to her actions, she assured him that she still wanted to see him. Richard interpreted her statement as a hopeful sign that somehow she was still emotionally connected to him. Therefore, if he was patient, she might resume the relationship with him.

It sounded as though Jackie, just twenty-two years old, wanted her freedom. She was good enough to stay with Richard while he was ill, but once he got better she moved to break up with him. She was direct about stating that she needed a break from the relationship, but when he complained and she saw how hurt he was, she tried to make things better by seeing him once a week. Maybe she wanted to keep Richard around until she found a better boyfriend. I never talked to Jackie myself, so I don't know how she felt. I was connecting the dots of information Richard gave me, and this is what I came up with.

I wondered how Richard would piece things together.

"Sounds like Jackie continues to say she wants you in her life, but her behaviors indicate she wants her freedom. And that is confusing to you," I said. "What do you think it all means?"

"I think she might want to end the relationship altogether. But she is afraid to say it because she doesn't want to feel badly about hurting me. She knows I don't want to hear it. She thinks I would rather she lie to me. So she is giving me a few hours of her time every Saturday. Or maybe she wants me to get fed up with her so that I break up with her. Maybe that's why she slept at the frat house and then told me about it. She wanted me to say that I've had it and we are through."

"So which way do you hurt more, Richard? If Jackie continues to do all this? Or if she breaks up with you and makes it stick? It looks like you are going to be hurting either way."

"Yes, it looks like it, but I would rather she tell me the truth. I would believe her this time."

Jackie's contradiction between words and behaviors is typical of the situation in which a person does not want to say the truth outright. Richard learned this the hard way. Eventually, he and Jackie broke up, and Richard moved on with his life.

Donna Requests and Gets
Information from her Fiancé's Ex-Wife

Verification can be as simple as going online and finding the information you need. Other times it is more complicated, especially when the only way to verify is to talk to other people.

Sometimes when I think a client of mine can benefit from it, I recommend that they contact the most recent ex of the person that they are seeing. I propose this to my client if special information is needed that cannot be obtained any other way.

I suggest such a meeting when I sense that a client may be making a big mistake. For example, if a girlfriend told my male client that she divorced her husband because he cheated on her, I do not necessarily take this at face value. What if they were not getting along? What if she cheated on him instead but does not want to say it? What if the girlfriend was lying to look good? The way to get the answer is to get the husband's side of the story. In Donna's case, I recommended that she talk with her fiancé's ex-wife.

Donna described how her fiancé had started to drink heavily. When Donna brought this to his attention and asked him to cut back on his drinking, his response was that he was only drinking more now because the wedding was getting closer and it was bringing up bad memories of his first marriage.

People who know little about alcoholics usually accept this excuse. However, anyone who knows alcoholics realizes that alcoholics, like any type of addict, often lie. If the lie works, they use it over and over again to cover their addiction. Donna's fiancé's lie is typical of the type of lie that an alcoholic would use. Therapists who specialize in the treatment of alcoholism and drug addiction are familiar with it, but Donna was too inexperienced with addicts to understand this. That meant I needed to enlighten her.

"Balderdash! That sounds like an excuse to me," I declared.

"You really think so?" Donna seemed amazed by my response. "Well, if it is untrue, how can I get at the truth? I don't want to marry an alcoholic."

"We have some options for getting at the truth. First of all, do you know the name of your fiancé's ex-wife and where she lives?"

"Yes."

"Well, what you could do is to call her, explain who you are, and what your concern is. Say that you are in need of her help and ask if she would meet you for coffee somewhere. Then ask her about your fiancé and whether he drank much during their marriage. While you're at it, ask her why their marriage broke up. It would be good to get her perspective."

"This is kind of weird." Donna was more shocked than amazed this time. "It sounds so intrusive. I never heard of anyone doing this before."

"If you call the lady and she does not wish to talk to you, I am sure she will say so. But most of the time people are very willing to help once they understand your situation. My guess is that she will talk with you."

Then I stayed silent while Donna hesitated. It looked as though she would reject the suggestion, but then she said, "I'll try it. God knows I have to try something. I'll invite her for coffee. Maybe it will help me somehow."

At our next therapy session, Donna looked sad and subdued. She said she had had a lengthy conversation with her fiancé's ex-wife.

"She is a very nice woman," Donna said. "When I said I needed her help, she was ready to give it. We met for coffee. I said I was engaged to her former husband but that I did not want to make a mistake. I asked her to tell me what in her mind caused the breakup of their marriage."

"Good for you for having the guts to do this. What did you find out?"

"First of all, I'm glad you suggested that I meet this lady in person. By meeting her in the flesh, I could size her up; you know what I mean? I saw that she was a nice and decent woman. I felt that she was telling me the truth."

Donna continued, "Now for the bad part. She said that he had been drinking for a very, very long time. He drank all the time, not just when he was stressed. When he was stressed it was worse. Their marriage broke up because he would not get help for his drinking. She said she had loved him very much, but he was setting a bad example for the children. And she could not have that."

We were silent. Donna was struggling to decide what to do with this information. She had a tough decision to make. Eventually, she started talking again. "First, I want to give him one last chance to go to a good detoxification program, then rehab, and AA. I now believe that he should have done that years ago. But if he refuses to do that, I have to get out. I am going to be very upset, but I will have to find a way out of my engagement. Can you help me?"

"Yes, of course," I said. Then I saw Donna's hands relax and come to rest in her lap.

Her fiancé promised he'd go for help. Donna waited for a year, but he never went. After that, Donna asked me to assist her in moving on with her life.

15

DETAILS OF SELF-PRESENTATION

Success is the sum of details.

Harvey S. Firestone,
of Firestone Tires

Before you start meeting people, take stock of your strengths and weaknesses in detail. Details are important to your self-presentation. People notice details.

For example, be prepared to talk about yourself in some detail. You need to be able to talk about LIFE topics (introduced in chapter three), as well as your strengths and weaknesses as a person. This is important, because as you meet people and ask them questions, they will also ask questions about you. So you will have to talk about yourself, and if you have prepared yourself for such conversations, you should make a good impression.

While the content of your speech is very important, so is your attitude toward yourself and others. Your having a positive attitude is another important detail. If someone asks you about yourself, take it as a compliment. That person is taking time out of their life to talk to you because they want to get to know you. Even if you do not care that a person is interested in you, be courteous. Do your best to answer in an accurate and pleasant manner, if only because that is who you are as a person. What you say and how you say it makes an impression that will be repeated to others. It is in your interest that people talk positively about you.

If you get negative feedback, try to correct the part of your presentation that reasonable people find objectionable. Do not take the criticism to heart. No one is perfect; everyone has advantages and disadvantages. What does matter is that you make an effort to improve yourself and your presentation of yourself.

The following stories emphasize the importance of these details.

Two Eligible Men with Different Attitudes Present Themselves to Jane

Jane worked hard on developing her screening criteria and decided to join an introductory dating service. It cost her money, but she was getting results. During her therapy sessions she compared the attitudes of two men she had met.

"I went to a singles' event for young professionals," Jane said. "A good-looking man asked me to dance. It happened to be a slow dance. I accepted his invitation but was put off by how closely he was holding me. I felt it was inappropriate. So I said so, in a nice way."

"What was his response to your saying that?"

"Well, he didn't like it one bit. He said, 'You know, I come from a prominent family, and I go to this prestigious private grad school. You could do worse than dance with me.' Then he held me close to him again. He implied that his exalted background should be good enough for me and that I should let him rub himself against me."

"How did you respond to that?"

"I was a little confused at first. I did not know how to respond. He certainly met my criteria on appearance and having a good education. Of course, a guy like that could be lying, but I just assumed he wasn't because the introduction service checks everyone out."

Jane continued, "But then I thought of his attitude, his audacity. He was disrespectful to me. Who does he think he is? God's gift to womankind? I don't care if he was having a bad day or something. I don't want anyone who is that full of himself."

I nodded. "It sounds like you were being true to yourself, Jane. What happened next?"

"I had this sense of wanting to leave, to get out of dancing with him. I wondered how to do it. Well, I wasn't going to educate him about how repulsive I found his attitude. I'm not his mother. So I just said, 'This isn't working for me,' and left the dance floor. He was amazed."

Undeterred by this experience, Jane kept going to dances. About a month later she came into my office with an extra bounce to her step.

"It has happened! I met a new man. We were introduced, and he took an interest in me. He asked me all about myself, and I asked him some things. We talked throughout the evening. He was easy to talk to; although, he is a little reserved."

"Did you have a chance to discuss your screening criteria?"

"Oh, yes." Jane was beaming. "His name is Jim. In education and family background he is similar to the other fellow I told you about last month. But the similarity ends there. Jim's attitude is low-key, respectful, quietly self-confident. He never boasted. I found out about his background by asking questions. Then I asked him how he felt about the advantages given him by his family and schooling."

"Good for you. How did he respond, and what did you think of it?"

"All he said was, 'I was fortunate,' and then changed the conversation to another topic. I liked that. When I think of Jim and the first guy, I am amazed. Their backgrounds were the same, but their attitudes could not have been more different."

Jane was silent for some time. "Doctor, I just cannot believe my good luck. Here is a man who meets my criteria with a good attitude, and he likes me. How did I get so lucky?"

"Jane, your hard work had something to do with it too. You paid attention to the details. You did not give up on finding a good man."

"Sometimes I despaired," Jane said. "I despaired that I would find a man who had all the details I was looking for. Then along came Jim. Thanks for encouraging me to keep looking. After that first man I was so upset that I almost gave up."

Jane's own good attitude and attention to detail led to her success.

The Details of Pete Trying to Meet Women

"I put in twelve hours a day at work," my client Pete explained. "Then I go to the gym. I have a light supper, watch a little TV, and go to sleep. On weekends I may have to work, but I try to make time for my sports league and parents. The bottom line is that all last year I did not meet a single eligible woman."

One night Pete had had enough. He decided to join one of the online dating services.

"I was fine with using the technology; although, it felt strange at first."

"How did you present yourself?" I asked. "What information about yourself did you put out there?"

"I was very low-key and careful. I did not want to say that I was an attorney, for obvious reasons. I did not put up good photos of myself for fear that one of my associates or clients might recognize me. I don't want them knowing my personal business. So I stated my hobbies and said I was looking for a committed relationship. That is how I presented myself."

"How are you doing meeting people?"

"It's mixed. It takes time to sort through messages and write back to the people I want to. Maybe I am too cautious, but I have to weigh my words and write exactly what I want to say. I have to be very careful about what I put online. Once it's out there, you never know where that e-mail might end up. So anyway, it is taking too much time.

"It's the same with phone calls. The only time I can really call people on the phone is in the evening before my bedtime. The problem with that is I stay up thinking about what people said. Then it takes me a long time to get to sleep."

The good news was that he was meeting women, so he was farther ahead than he had been the year before. The bad news was that sometimes the women were not as advertised. For example, the posted photos showed a much more attractive woman than she presented in the flesh. Other times a woman would tell Pete that she was divorced, but once out to dinner with her, Pete would learn that she was only separated.

The details of online dating were not working for Pete.

"Well, I am meeting women," Pete summarized, "but I am not meeting anyone I want to keep seeing."

The next time I saw him, Pete explained that he had contacted a professional dating service. "I got a bonus at work, so I decided, what the heck, I will try a more expensive professional service. My parents were all for it. I set up an appointment."

I did not see Pete for two months, as he had to travel for work and I went on vacation. At our next appointment, he eased into my armchair and smiled.

"Let me update you on my dating life, Doctor. First of all, this service is rigorous."

"How do you mean, Pete?"

"Well, I had a pre-qualifying phone interview and saw a professional counselor. Then I took personality and compatibility tests, and they ran a CORI [criminal offender record information] check on me. In a personal interview I was asked for my screening criteria, which, thanks to my work with you, I had ready to give them. They emphasized that I needed to be legally and emotionally single, which of course I am. After this I was told that I seemed to have a good attitude and that my criteria were realistic. They would send me a referral. To protect everyone's privacy, there would be no photo or e-mail exchanges. I would just be given a women's first name and phone number to call, and she would be given mine.

"Next, the counselor commented on my physical appearance. She said I needed to maintain better eye contact when speaking, stand up straight, and send my clothes to the cleaner's more often. I was pretty offended."

"That is all true, Pete," I said.

"Really? Well, if you think so too…"

"Those little things are important. I wish I had mentioned them myself," I said, a little embarrassed. "Those details send the message that you have pride enough to attend to your appearance. Looking people in the eye, for example, signals that you are self-confident. The people you meet notice those things."

"I see your point. I never thought of it in the context of meeting women, but I myself notice these things when I work with clients and other attorneys. I always make it a point to look good in the courtroom."

The next time I saw Pete, he had already met a few referrals.

"How are you doing, Pete?"

"The women I met were fine," Pete said in a relaxed manner, "and one appears to be special. Guess what?"

"What?"

"She is a practicing attorney, and she also struggled with online dating first."

"What do you think?"

"I am thinking about it."

"I have not ever heard you say that before, Pete. How serious are you?"

"Well, I may be way ahead of myself, but I know I can say whatever I want in here. So I'll say it. I am wondering how it would work out, two working attorneys raising a family together."

"So this lady is a keeper from what you see so far?"

"So far. But I have only had a few dates with her. The potential may be there, for marriage, I mean."

"How does she do in meeting your criteria?"

"Well, it is interesting. The service must have listened to my criteria when they interviewed me, because she seems to check out on most. The rest I will have to ask about. But I want to move slowly; I don't want to get my hopes up."

Pete continued, "What I really want to do is to meet her family somehow. They live about thirty miles away. That is the detail I really want to check on. But how can I invite myself over there? Do you have any ideas?"

"Let's see. Why don't you lead by example?" I asked. "How about inviting your parents to your house and have the lady drop in for coffee?

"Usually I would recommend a restaurant for the meeting," I continued. "But since you already know her well enough, it's fine to invite her to your house. Also, her coming to your house to meet your parents would set the psychological stage for you to be invited to her parents' home. Then you would not only meet her parents but also see the house they live in and maybe some other details of their family life."

Pete was listening, so I continued, "In other words, you do what you would like her to do. If she is bright and understands that you think well enough of her to have her meet your parents, she will probably reciprocate and extend an invitation for you to meet her folks."

"Yeah, okay," Pete agreed. "Even if it doesn't happen that way, it is worth seeing what comes of it."

Thankfully, it all worked out. His parents liked the lady very well. To his delight, Pete received an invitation to meet the woman's parents. Her parents were very nice and seemed to like him. A little later, Pete said he was all set and terminated therapy.

16

⤜⧽⧼⤛

MOVING TOWARD HAPPINESS: UNDERSTANDING DISADVANTAGES

If your ship does not come in, swim out to meet it.

Jonathan Winters,
American comedian

Laura Changes for the Better but Struggles with Self-Worth

Twenty-two-year-old Laura presented herself as a strong person and devout Christian of good family background. Her only problem was depression. She sought the assistance of her preacher, but he was not able to help. She called me because she had seen online that I was a provider for her health insurance and she liked the sound of my name.

"I am rarely happy," Laura said. "I see that other people are happy and that seems like fun. How can I be happy?"

"Tell me about yourself, Laura, and maybe we can figure it out."

I ask a lot of questions in the initial interview because in my profession it is my business to get to know a person as quickly as possible. Laura was forthcoming in answering and even appeared grateful that she could talk about herself. Before asking about her family background, I wanted to know what her typical day was like and whether she was getting enough sleep.

My reason for asking about her sleep pattern was that if she was not getting enough sleep, as many young people do not, that could be a contributing factor to her depression. By asking about her sleep, I learned a lot about Laura's whole life, including her family.

"How is your sleep, Laura? Are you getting eight hours each night?"

"Not really."

"What keeps you from getting eight hours of sleep?"

"Many things. Sometimes I have to babysit my sister's little boy because I live with them. Several nights I go out after work to hang out with friends and my boyfriend. He works odd hours, so I go to see him when he calls."

"When does he get off of work?"

"He usually calls around two a.m. That is when he wants to see me, and I go out to meet him."

"When do you get to sleep before that time?"

"It depends on what's going on each night. But I am usually asleep by midnight."

By now I realized that Laura was not getting enough sleep, so lack of sleep could be contributing to her depression. Why was she going out in the middle of the night? I soon found out.

"I sleep from midnight to whenever John calls; then I go out and see him," Laura explained. "We hang out and have sex. Then I go back to bed at about four a.m. and get to my job at the newspaper by eight a.m."

"Doesn't John feel badly that he is interrupting your sleep?"

"I don't think so."

"What do your mother and sister think about your going out to see John in the middle of the night?"

"Oh, they love John. They think I should do whatever I can to keep him. And if I complain about him sometimes, they always take his side and tell me to fix the problem."

"What makes John so special? Is he a really great guy?"

"He's just a guy. He pays attention to me."

"Are you in love with him? Do you plan to marry?"

"No, we never talk about that. Besides, I don't get the concept of marriage."

"You don't get the concept of marriage?"

"No. Of what benefit is marriage to me?"

As Laura continued in therapy, I found out more and more about how she grew up. She basically raised herself and was emotionally alone. Her mother and father were elderly and disabled, living separately but nearby, never married. Laura's older sister had an eight-year-old son by a man who had another girlfriend and children and who rarely came to visit. Laura was living with the sister and her nephew rent-free in exchange for extensive babysitting. Laura loved all of her family but could not remember a time when they had all lived together.

Although she considered herself a devout Christian, marriage was not a sacrament she ever heard of. Through the example of her mother and sister, Laura concluded that marriage was not a part of family life. Her sister did not expect her boyfriend to marry her, even when their child was born. While having children out of wedlock seemed normal, it bothered Laura that the boy's father rarely came to visit.

Since this upset Laura, I decided to ask about her views on parenting responsibilities. What did she think her sister's boyfriend should be doing to make things right?

"He should be raising his son. He should be visiting a lot. He should be giving my sister a little money for his son's upkeep."

I decided to try to describe why I thought things were the way they were.

"Laura, I am not surprised that the father does nothing. He was never held to high standards by your sister."

"What standards are you talking about? What do you mean?"

"Well, it sounds like your sister did not expect much out of him. She let him get away with things. She did not expect marriage to begin with. Then she had a child with him and did not sue for child support. She is not making him walk the line and do his job by his son. He gets away with fooling around with another woman and ignoring his son."

"You are mentioning marriage again," Laura said. "What is marriage anyway? It's just a piece of paper, as far as I know."

"Well, some people think marriage is much more than a piece of paper," I said gently. "That piece of paper is a sign of the commitment two people make to each other. The commitment is to stand by each other, to love and support each other, to live and to raise children together. Marriage is intended to be forever."

Laura was listening, so I kept talking. "That piece of paper means other things too. It has legal meaning. The institution of marriage provides legal and financial protection for the wife and children. And then, most importantly, if your preacher marries you, it has Christian meaning. It means God blessed your union in marriage."

I could tell Laura was hearing these ideas for the first time, so I added just one more thought.

"If a man is not willing to have children with a woman inside the bounds of marriage, a woman does not have to have him. Actually, why bother with him? There are men who are strong enough to commit to a family and stay loyal to it. Also, it is better for the children to have both parents around. Just like you said, your nephew's father should be there to raise his son and pay for expenses. Instead of that, your sister is trying to do the job of two parents all by herself."

Laura seemed a little shocked but continued in therapy. For the next few years I saw her on and off as her need to talk with me came and went. She started taking night courses and did not see her boyfriend as often as before. Their relationship ebbed and flowed. At one point she moved in with him because her sister asked her to leave the apartment to make room for the boy's father (who had gotten kicked out by his girlfriend).

Laura was promoted at work and finished her associate's degree with the financial assistance of her workplace. She seemed happier. She bought her first new car. She was proud of herself. When she thought to look for a better job so she could pay off some debts, I supported her efforts. There was a job opening in a city ten miles away, with a good highway leading to it. However, Laura would not call for an interview. She was terrified of the drive.

"I would not know how to get there," she explained. "I never go far from home. My church just moved away because the rent went up, and I can't even make myself go to service."

"How about we think of strategies to get you there? How about we find some really clear directions to the address of the company that has the job?"

"I don't think I can do it," Laura protested. "Really, I can't."

I backed off. By this time I knew Laura would move forward only when she was ready and had had a lot of time to think things over. Some months later, Laura called me in a panic. She needed to talk right away. Her anxiety was that work was making her travel to the Philippines.

I understood that she was scared, but I wanted to point out that the trip would be great for her confidence and personal growth.

"I don't even know where the Philippines are." Laura was trembling from the nervousness. "But work told me I have to go. The newspaper is losing money, and they are relocating the call center there. I have to train the women in the Philippines how to take calls."

"Well, Laura, good for you! Look at it this way: you get to travel, and work pays for it. You'll do all right. Enjoy yourself, okay?"

Laura forced a smile. "I hope so. You should have seen me when work asked me if they should rent a car for me to drive in the Philippines. I just about fainted! Me driving in the Philippines? I can't even drive here. So they said I could take taxis. That made me feel better."

Laura's therapy is a work in progress. She called to say she had a great time in the Philippines and she was happy. She signed up for a legal secretary course because she decided her newspaper was not going to make it, and she wanted to prepare herself to work in a law office.

From the time she started therapy, Laura made many changes in her life. She took her time making them, but the changes were real. She decided to get eight straight hours of sleep at night and to act in her own best interest. Another change was that she started to expect that a boyfriend of hers should do things for her, not just her doing things for him. Her depression slowly lifted.

While Laura is still struggling with issues of self-worth, especially with respect to men, she feels happier and more self-confident. She has more faith in her future. She's even started work on her acceptance criteria, because she might like to get married someday.

Susie Likes a Man with a Dysfunctional Background

What if a person meets all of your screening criteria except that of family background? What if the family background is dysfunctional? What do you do? Does it mean a marriage with this person will not work?

My client Susie struggled with these questions. Overall, she really liked Steve. He appeared to be a fine person and met her criteria, except for the family background.

"To sum it up," Susie was explaining, "Steve's father abandoned him and his mother. Steve doesn't think his father even knew his mom was pregnant with him. Then his mother died of a drug overdose when he was eleven years old, and Steve was raised by his grandparents. That is a problem for me. Also, Steve is an only child, which I also said I did not want. That is the bad news."

"The good news is the very close relationship between Steve and his grandparents," Susie continued. "And I think Steve himself would be a good mate. But I have to ask myself questions. How did Steve turn out so well? Can I trust this situation? Or should I move on and look for someone else?"

"Susie, I wish there were clear answers," I replied. "Before we think more about Steve's parents, let's back up a little. What makes you think Steve would be good for marriage?"

"Well, he meets my criteria. So far everything he said about himself is true. I have a relative who checked Steve out. He has good credit, graduated from college when he said he did, and has a good record at the company he works for. He is smart, considerate, and I am attracted to him. I am just trying to figure out how bad parents can produce as good of a person as Steve."

"So if Steve came from an intact family, you would marry him?"

"Absolutely. What I worry about is that he does not know how to be in a family. You know, like what his role as a husband and father would be."

"Perhaps you and Steve could talk about this."

"I can do that. But I want your opinion. You are the professional person whose ideas I want," Susie continued. "Have you ever seen a person from a dysfunctional family make a good spouse and parent?"

Of course I have. At this point I recalled the many fine people I have known over the years who came from hellish backgrounds but possessed fine personal qualities for marriage. Dysfunctional families can sometimes produce fine marital spouses, just as well-functioning families sometimes produce a dysfunctional child. I recalled the many only child persons, the orphans, and foster home children I knew. They grew up yearning to have a nice family of their own, and, when their turn came, they were very devoted to their spouse and family.

It was time to discuss what Susie knew about Steve's parents.

"First of all, is it possible that Steve's biological parents may not have been all bad?" I wondered. "Let's think about this. What if Steve's father did not know a baby was on the way? What if he left the relationship for other reasons? How did this happen? Does anyone know?"

Susie researched the family background by talking with the grandparents, who said they had liked Steve's father. He moved away after his relationship with their daughter broke up. Once Steve was born, their daughter never looked for Steve's father.

"If that is true, Steve's father may have been an okay person," I said. "If the father did not know that he impregnated Steve's mother, he may have left the relationship for other reasons. He cannot be blamed for the abandonment if he never knew that the pregnancy existed."

Susie nodded in agreement. "Yes, as far as I know there was no DNA testing. His mother never exercised her rights under the mandated child support payment laws. Very likely, she never told him of Steve's existence."

"Then we have Steve's mom dying from an accidental or intended drug overdose. Do you have any information on which it was, Susie?"

"Steve said his mom left a note. The overdose was a suicide. His mom was in love with someone who turned away from her. The mom could not accept the loss of the relationship and became depressed. Steve's grandparents tried to convince the mom to get help, but she wouldn't."

I thought this through and said, "What information do Steve's grandparents have of Steve's mother's history of drug usage?"

Apparently Susie had peppered Steve's grandparents with questions, because she had this information as well. "The grandparents told me there was not any drug use by Steve's mother that they knew of. There were never signs of drug-related activity such as being under the influence, missing items or money, losing jobs or hanging with druggies."

"What is most likely then is that Steve's mother had some kind of depression," I said. "It got worse, and she killed herself. That is the risk you are most likely looking at, Susie. We know that the predisposition to depression can be inherited, so there is a likelihood that as time goes on Steve may experience a depressive episode. There's also a chance that your children could have depression. However, depression is a treatable condition, and it does not have to be crippling to a marriage, parenthood, or a career."

"What are the symptoms?" Susie asked, so we talked about that. (Anyone can access this information by researching the topic, so I will not review the symptoms here.)

Once we finished I asked Susie, "Have you noticed any signs of depression in Steve at this point?"

She was thoughtful for a moment. "No, I can't say that I have. I've known Steve for two years now, and I haven't seen it."

Susie continued, "Steve is a lot like his grandparents. I feel comfortable with all three of them. I am thinking now that Steve's grandparents are his parents. When I think of it like that, he comes from a well-functioning family."

I commented that Steve was lucky to have a nice, capable set of grandparents to make a family for him.

"Yes," Susie agreed. "And he certainly made the most of his life. When I think of it, he does not act like an only child. I guess I can accept the idea that sometimes weird things happen in life. My own parents raised me, and I count myself lucky. Not everyone is so fortunate. At least Steve has nice grandparents. If Steve and I work together, I think we can make a happy future for ourselves. I am willing to run the risk that he might get depressed sometime in the future."

Susie was smiling. She seemed pleased with her emerging decision to have Steve in her life. We left it at that.

About five years later I bumped into Susie at the grocery store checkout line. I usually do not get into the same checkout line as a client of mine if I recognize the client first. That day I did not notice Susie, as she was bent over emptying her grocery cart in front of me. I acted as if I had not noticed her, which, as I explain to all my clients, is my standard policy in case I meet them in a public place. This is how I act in order to protect their confidentiality of having been in therapy with me. By not saying hello first, I cause no inconvenience, such as their having to explain to someone else who I am and how they know me.

The majority of my former clients remember this and choose to say hello.

Susie did too, very casually.

I looked at her, and she smiled. Then I saw the wedding band on her left ring finger and the handsome, quiet little boy sitting in the shopping cart.

"This is my little boy, Steve," Susie said to me. The wide, loving smile she gave her child is one I will always remember.

I smiled back at them and said hello to little Steve.

17

THE HELP OF TRUSTED FAMILY MEMBERS

Advice is like snow; the softer it falls, the longer it
dwells upon and the deeper it sinks into the mind.

Samuel Taylor Coleridge

In general, women can size up other women better than men can.
Similarly, men are better evaluators of other men than women
are. I call this "same-sex evaluation" and recommend it to my clients. For example, I regularly suggest that a single man introduce
the woman he is dating to trusted female relatives and get their
feedback. I also encourage single women to get the opinions of
trusted male relatives concerning the man you are considering
for marriage.

Most single people do not seek the opinion of same-sex evaluators. Worse, not only do they not ask for feedback, they disregard it when it is offered. This was what Robert did. When I first
met him, he was tense and angry.

Robert Should Have Listened to His Mother

"My wife of one year left me," he announced to me, "and she took a car and all the money from our bank account. What she did leave behind was a huge charge card debt."

We talked for several sessions about how hurt he was and whether he wanted to try to reconcile with his wife. In one conversation he mentioned that his parents were upset by the news.

I asked him something that I typically ask of my clients with relationship problems: "Robert, before you got engaged, did you ever ask your parents for their opinion of your wife?"

"No, I never did."

"Did your parents volunteer any opinion of her before you married?"

"No." Robert said, but he checked himself and paused for a minute. "Well, yes. I remember my mother mentioning that she did not seem as honest as the girlfriend I had before."

"What was your reaction to your mother's comment at that time?

"I just shrugged it off."

"Did you at any time ask your mother what she meant by that comment? It could have been her way of starting a conversation with you."

"No, although now I wish I had. But I was only twenty-one. My attitude was that I knew better. Mom was just butting in. But you know what? If there is a next time, I will listen to her."

Robert's mother picked up on something important about Robert's former wife that Robert did not notice. It is possible that his mother tried to be helpful and communicate a caution to her son. Unfortunately for Robert, he did not listen. Parents often notice things and try to forewarn their children. Although he did not listen when he was twenty-one years old, he now realized that he had a friend in his mother. Next time Robert would ask her opinion.

Family interventions are needed in circumstances where unexpected and previously unknown information has been received and needs to be passed on. The following is a story from many years ago. It was the first time I witnessed a family intervention.

Caroline's Father Intervenes to Stop Her Marriage

Caroline was an army nurse stationed overseas. Although many young officers wanted to date her, she socialized off base with Vietnamese people. Eventually she fell in love with an attractive and cultured local man. Caroline was impressed by the man's knowledge of languages, his charm, and sophistication. He wooed her with elegance, persistence, and devotion. She decided he was the right man for her.

As it happened, Caroline's father was also stationed in that country as a high-ranking military officer, and Caroline's intimate socializing with a foreign national created a very real security concern. If any sensitive military information were transmitted from father to daughter, it was possible that the lover could hear of it and use that to the detriment of the soldiers fighting the war. As a matter of routine security practice, a background investigation was initiated on Caroline's lover.

As the security investigation was taking place, Caroline told her father that her lover had proposed marriage and that she wanted to accept his offer. She hoped this was okay with her father. She also said her lover would be happy to return with her to live in the States, whenever Caroline decided to move back home. The father said that was fine with him.

Caroline started her wedding preparations, choosing a quiet ecumenical service. A few days before the marriage, her father received the completed security report. His heart sank as he read it. The report documented that Caroline's fiancé already had a wife and children.

It was the father's sad duty to break the news to his daughter. Caroline's anguish was acute, and she could hardly believe her ears. Her lover had never mentioned a wife or children. Of course, she had never thought to ask. She assumed that he was single like herself. How could this have happened?

Her fiancé tried to explain. He said he was rich enough to support two wives and claimed that in his culture and religion he was allowed to have more than one wife. Caroline was too upset to find out if this was true. Her happiness was destroyed; she felt duped.

Marriage was now out of the question. As an American woman, she could not imagine being anyone's second wife. Besides, polygamy was not allowed in the United States. What had her fiancé been planning for after the wedding? That he would marry Caroline and when they moved to the States he would send for his first wife and children? Or did he plan to abandon his first family and leave his children behind? Either was unbearable for Caroline to think about and completely unacceptable.

She again questioned her fiancé, who said that it was all a cultural misunderstanding.

Caroline was very sad, and her father worried about her. In the end, Caroline thanked her father for sharing the contents of the security report. Looking back on it today, she feels that her father and the report saved her from a making a terrible mistake.

Sarita's Parents Find
Men and Do Background Checks Besides

In many world cultures and some US subcultures parents select their children's spouses. This is a religious/cultural practice transported from the old country and applied to offspring in the United States.

Sarita's story is that of an arranged marriage. She initially consulted me about work-related stress, but at one point I had reason to ask if she had an arranged marriage. She said she did and told me how her marriage came about. It is very different from the hands-off approach of our mainstream American dating and marriage patterns, especially in how much the parents work to find a suitable person for marriage.

When Sarita was young, her parents told her she did not have to worry about dating or marriage. Her parents would find her a good husband when the time was right. Sarita accepted her parents' decision to withhold her from American dating patterns. She accepted her parents' guidance that her job was to get good grades in school, go to a good college, and get a degree so she could make a good income. This was the way, her parents said, to attract a good husband and have a good marriage.

When Sarita graduated from college, her mother asked her if she was ready to marry. Since she was not sure, her parents encouraged her to think about it. Then her mother asked her if there was any man she met in college that she liked. If there was such a man, her mother explained, her parents would research him first to see if he met their criteria and was a suitable match.

Sarita replied that there was no one like that. A year later, she felt ready to become someone's wife. She gave her parents the go-ahead to find her a husband. In Sarita's case, the search was worldwide. There are one million or so members of their Christian Hindu church living inside and outside of India. Family and friendship ties span several continents. Sarita's parents used their connections to locate eligible Christian Hindu men who met specific acceptance and rejection screening criteria.

"What acceptance and rejection screening criteria did your parents have?" I asked her.

"The ones I would have," Sarita replied. "An educated man with a good career, of my religion, with polite manners. Oh, and our parents would have to be able to get along."

"Why would your parents have to get along with each other?"

"Well, it's hard to explain. But if our parents are too different, then we would probably not have a good marriage."

What was "too different" was left vague. Sarita implied that social class differences, poor physical presentation, lack of cleanliness, poor manners, and primitive speech patterns by the man's parents were unacceptable. These appeared to be her parents' rejection criteria.

"Sarita, did you have anything to say about who you would marry?"

"Yes, I did. My parents would never force me to marry against my will. I had a choice among the men they eventually introduced me to."

Sarita said she recognized all the work and expense her parents put into finding her a husband. She knew which man she wanted for a husband right when she met him. Since her parents had cleared the young man in terms of acceptance and rejection criteria, she felt relaxed and comfortable with him. She had some un-chaperoned dates with her fiancé before the marriage.

I asked how her marriage was going. She said it was fine.

"Were you in love with your fiancé before you married him?"

"I was comfortable with him. In our culture, being in love before marriage is not desirable."

"Where does love come into the relationship with your husband?" I asked.

"My parents told me that love comes after marriage, once it is deserved. Love will come because I married a deserving man of my background. Love will come if I work at the marriage. Love will come if he was raised well by his parents, which he was, and if I am a good wife. I have been that, and we love each other."

Sarita continued, "It is not a perfect marriage. What attracted me to him first now irritates me. He was reserved and did not talk much when I met him. He is still that way; I want him to talk to me more. But I love and respect him. He is a fine person and makes good money. We are in complete agreement on how to raise the children. And I keep in mind that no marriage is perfect."

"Do people of your background ever divorce?"

"More now than before. But for us, it is more complicated. If we divorce, we bring shame on our parents, ourselves, and our children. It would mean that our parents did not do their screening job well. If we have marital problems, we are expected to work them out. We talk with our parents and trusted relatives and listen to their advice. He talks with his parents, and I confide in mine. They advise us on what to do, and we follow the advice."

What a different process this is from what Western singles go through! Sarita did not have to search for a husband because her parents acted as a sophisticated screening and matchmaking service, even to the point of evaluating the man's parents. Sarita had her pick of eligible men without having to spend the time and money to locate them. She also did not have safety issues to be concerned about.

Would she be happier with someone else? She does not waste time thinking about it. She believes she has a good marriage. Besides, she would never divorce her husband because that would put her children at a disadvantage when it came to be their time to marry.

In contrast to the way Sarita married, mainstream American singles are very independent indeed. They rarely seek their parents' opinion on who to marry. The next case describes how a mother finally got tired of her son's marital choices and decided to speak up.

Ruth Gives Her Son Advice
before He Marries for the Third Time

I was treating Ruth for post-traumatic stress disorder (PTSD) from a serious car accident. At sixty-seven years of age, Ruth appeared to be patient, capable, and in overall good health. But as the treatment progressed, she did not appear any happier. Instead, she always seemed tired and worn out.

At the time of history taking, Ruth only mentioned problems with PTSD symptoms, so I was puzzled. I kept asking her what the matter was. One day Ruth decided to tell me.

"I hate to talk like this," Ruth began, "but I'm upset due to the children."

"What children, Ruth? I thought your children were all grown up."

"My son's children, my grandchildren. I feel like I am a bad grandmother to complain at all. But since you keep asking me, Dr. O'Hara, and since you helped me with the PTSD, I thought maybe I should tell you."

"I'd be happy to listen, Ruth. Please let me know what is troubling you about the grandchildren."

"These children have been through a lot. I want them to make my home their home, but I just don't know if I can do it. They need my help, but I don't know if I can give it," Ruth said and burst into tears. "I just feel awful about it.

"What happened is this," Ruth said when she had composed herself. "My son has always been attracted to the wrong type of woman. Maggie and Johnny are my son's young children from his second marriage. They all lived in Florida, and I knew there were problems. I did not know how bad these problems were until my son's former wife was arrested for buying drugs while she left one of the children in the car. Before that, a social worker came to the house and found the children playing alone in the yard while their mother was sleeping off a hangover. The court awarded physical and legal custody of the children to my son, with the understanding that my son's family would help take care of them."

Ruth continued, "Then my son moved the children up here to live with me. Mind you, I invited them. I take care of them by myself. My son has to keep working in Florida for another year to finish his contract, and then, he says, he'll look for work here. But the way my son is, I don't know if he will follow through. In the meantime, I am exhausted trying to take care of the children. Isn't that an awful thing to say, Doctor? I am sure that you think worse of me for it."

I tried to reassure Ruth. "I think you are a very nice and kind person, Ruth. I know you want nothing but the best for your grandchildren. Of course you get tired; I think anyone would. In a normal role as grandmother, you would be seeing them a few times a week, which you could handle very well. But instead of that, you are doing all the work that their mother and father should be doing. No wonder you are exhausted."

Ruth looked relieved, so I continued, "I'd like to back up a little. You said you did not know if your son would ever move up here to work and help you raise his children. What do you mean by that?"

"What I mean is that he is so stupid sometimes. He always goes for the wrong women. It's like he does not think. So if he meets another woman in Florida while he is working out his contract, I may be raising these children forever. Of course I love them, and they need me. They might as well be orphans, though."

"Ruth, have you ever told your son what you just told me?"

"Oh, no. I couldn't."

"What do you mean you couldn't? You are raising his children for him. He owes you a great deal. How come you couldn't?"

"I know, I know. But growing up he never asked for my opinion, and I never gave it."

"Well, it might be helpful for both of you if you changed that pattern. It's never too late to give your opinion, is it?"

"But I couldn't, I'm just not brave enough."

"Ruth, let me put it this way. Maybe if you nicely share with your son what you are thinking, he will understand your concern. Maybe in the future he will select a different type of woman. He has every reason to listen to you now, especially since he is so indebted to you. What's the harm in trying to talk to him? On the other hand, if you don't talk to him, he might get married to the same type of woman a third time, and five years from now you may have yet another grandchild to raise. Can you picture yourself raising three grandchildren?"

Ruth visibly collapsed in her armchair. I felt badly for her. Perhaps I made my point too strongly. "Look, Ruth, I'm sorry I said it so plainly. I don't mean to upset you, but I owe it to you to tell you what I am thinking."

Ruth nodded in understanding.

Shortly after this, Ruth proposed that she bring her son, Nick, into our therapy sessions. Ruth wanted me present when she talked to him about his choice in women. Nick came up from Florida on a short visit and appeared pleased to be invited to our session. He seemed at ease.

Ruth started the session by expressing her anxiety about being strong enough to raise the children by herself.

Nick was quick to respond. "Oh, no, Mom. I am definitely moving up here. They are my children, and I want to raise them."

"Nick, you say that now, but I am scared that something will happen. What if you meet another woman?"

"What do you mean, Mom?"

"Nick, you know I love you very much, and I never said anything ever about your choice in women, but Dr. O'Hara here feels that I should somehow say to you what's on my mind."

Nick looked at me and then at to his mother. "Mom, I would welcome your ideas. Especially if you could tell me something helpful so I don't marry the wrong person again."

"Okay. Please, just think through what I say first. I love you so much. What I see, Nick, is that twice you married poorly. How come that happened?"

"Mom, you are right. I have twice proposed marriage based on physical attraction. I am clearly attracted to the wrong type. Once I am attracted, I stop thinking. I made two big mistakes."

"What went wrong in the marriages, Nick?" Ruth asked.

"Let's just say that both were drug addicts, only I was too dumb to know. I grew up in a very nice household, and I did not know much about women when I first married. My wives, when I met them, were the most attractive, vivacious, and sexy of women. I had no idea they were speeding, and that is what made them so attractive. They were both very good at hiding things. A year into both marriages I started to suspect that things were wrong. But I did not know what.

"Mom, I feel very badly about the children," Nick continued. "I've had time to think, and it is my fault. The children were damaged by their mother's drugging and drinking and by my being stupid. Mom, have you noticed how small my little girl is? At her age, she should be four inches taller than what she is. I now know that she was malnourished for years. And my son, he has learning disorders [LD]. There is no history of LD in our family, Mom. I think my son's LD comes from her drugging while she was pregnant with him. Mom, I am so sorry that I have failed to protect my children."

Nick and his mother were both crying by now. I passed the tissue box. I was pleasantly surprised at how well the conversation was going, especially since, by Ruth's account, they had never talked like this before. I stayed quiet while mother and son savored their closeness and dried their tears.

Eventually Ruth broke the silence. "Nick, my biggest fear is that you will meet another woman like that and you will be taken in again and have children with another such woman. I don't think I could bear it, all that sadness."

"Mom, I understand that. I am sorry for the sadness and work I have caused you. I promise you, I will not meet women until I move up here next year. I am going to put my energies into working out my contract and finding a job up here. If I have to take a demotion, a cut in pay, no matter what, I am moving up here. And once I am here, I am going to have the children live with me. I will date only after that, and I will bring the women by so you can meet them and give me your opinion of them. It is obvious to me that I need your input."

Ruth was smiling. Nick winked at his mother and said, "In front of Dr. O'Hara, our witness, if I don't keep my word, you may castrate me."

We laughed, enjoying the emotional relief of a joke after a serious, first-of-its kind discussion.

Ruth came alone to the next session. She seemed confident and happy. None of her depressive symptoms were evident.

"I am so glad I started talking to my son. I am thankful I could share with him what was in my heart. When we got home from the session we talked some more. It was so reassuring to me. I don't think he'll pick another hyper-druggie woman."

Ruth listened and was able to break the pattern of not talking with her son. Other parents can too. If you are a parent reading this, try to establish a nice pattern of talking with your child early on. Do not just talk about everyday things. Talk also about your hopes, fears, ideas, and observations of the people around you. Talking like this helps bring you closer to the children and teach them about life. Guide such conversations so they are positive, constructive encounters.

Sometimes, for one reason or another, this kind of communication does not take place while a child is growing up. Thus the child does not learn how to talk deeply with anyone. In Ruth and Nick's case, Nick's father left the family when Nick was young, and Ruth worked hard to raise Nick alone. Ruth thought she was doing a good job by providing Nick with the necessities of life, but she did not get into the habit of having conversations with him.

Not until Nick became a father himself and Ruth took care of his children did Ruth, out of desperation, break the cycle and start talking. Nick, as it turned out, was very willing and had a lot to say himself.

Ruth and Nick continued to talk. Their communication became more frequent. Nick finished his contract and moved back. Ruth no longer needed therapy.

It is never too late to start talking, especially when both parties are willing and able. There is a lot to talk about, especially when the topic is how to marry right!

Appendix A:

Acceptance and Rejection Criteria Contributed by Long-Married Couples and Health Care Professionals

Introduction

Acceptance criteria are positive characteristics a person has to have in order to be considered for marriage. Rejection criteria are negative characteristics you are looking for that may make the person with the characteristics unsuitable for marriage.

The purpose of these criteria is to provide a framework for decision-making about people (prior to becoming emotionally involved with them). By following these criteria, a person can avoid bad relationships and divorce. Your using these criteria will make it more likely that you will select a good spouse and have a stable, happy marriage.

A large number of people contributed their criteria for this book, but due to space limitations, only a few are included in this appendix. I wish to thank everyone who contributed.

You will notice that many of the criteria are retrospective. I mean by this that the criteria came from people who, looking back on their long lives, chose criteria that they judge to be most useful and important in the selection of a spouse. The criteria are retrospective from both the person's married experience as well as their professional roles as mental health workers or religious clergy.

I selected the following contributors to this Appendix because:

- They have been happily married to the same spouse for over twenty years or more

- They are professional mental health providers or clergy who counsel people

- They have advanced degrees in psychology, counseling, or closely related fields

- They practice and are guided by faith in their daily life

Criteria Suggested By Survey Participants

*Indicates people who did not provide rejection criteria.

Linda* is fifty-three years old and the mother of two grown children. When she spoke to me about her criteria, Linda and her husband were celebrating the twenty-fifth anniversary of their marriage. She is a businesswoman, singer, songwriter, and overseas mission preacher.

Linda's acceptance criteria:

1. come from a good family, with a nice mother and father

2. not be jealous or possessive

3. not violent and not yell or raise his voice

4. be accepting of my independence

5. be a hard worker

6. enjoy the outdoors

7. be a good listener

8. be able to see the beauty in things both simple and complex

9. have attention to detail

10. have no financial problems and be responsible with money

Deb is a forty-seven-year-old schoolteacher and has been married for twenty-four years to a businessman. Deb and her husband are close to their extended families. Their two children are now in college and come home to help out with property improvements.

DEB'S ACCEPTANCE CRITERIA:

1. strong morals and the ability to stand up for his beliefs

2. the sharing of many of the same interests

3. a willingness to live up to responsibilities

4. physically attractive

5. similar or identical financial thoughts and values

6. similar views on child rearing and parenting responsibilities-

7. demonstrate ability to work through disagreements

8. a personality that blends with mine

9. ability to commit for life

10. age of the person should be close enough for lifelong sharing of interests

DEB'S REJECTION CRITERIA:

1. a person without strong morals

2. a person known to be violent

3. an alcohol or drug user of any type

4. person who has no ambition

Melissa is a thirty-eight-year-old single woman who helps out her widowed mother and three nieces. She has a counseling degree and works in an urban community clinic. She is dating and available.

MELISSA'S ACCEPTANCE CRITERIA:

1. integrity—without this, their word is no good to anyone, especially me

2. honesty—if they are dishonest with others, they will be dishonest with me

3. ability to compromise—should not be stubborn, should be able to meet people halfway

4. is trustworthy without question

5. is motivated to improve himself in life and in the relationship

6. has a sense of humor—we must be able to laugh together

7. has the ability to listen—really listen, even when they've heard it before

8. be able to challenge me intellectually, emotionally, and spiritually

9. be productive—contribute to family, work steadily, take pride in accomplishments

10. be stable—in personal life, in job history, in past commitments that were made

11. creative—keep life interesting, look at fresh ideas, keep growing, don't stagnate

12. be kind—to everyone (how a person is toward others is how he will be toward me)

13. be independent—have the ability to start projects and see them through to completion

14. be happy—with himself and comfortable with who he is

15. saw how his parents worked out their problems and is willing to do it with me

16. has expectations of life similar to my own

MELISSA'S REJECTION CRITERIA:

1. anyone with an alcoholic or drug addiction past (too much potential for a relapse)

2. married more than once before—has a bad track record

3. sounds ignorant and is unable to articulate thoughts using proper grammar

4. unstable work history, unstable finances, unstable emotions

5. uneducated

6. a CORI (Criminal Offender Record Information) showing that he's been in trouble with the law

7. overly concerned with appearances and the attractiveness of companions

8. no potential for growth—stuck in his place in life and going nowhere

9. has children from previous relationships/marriages

10. fails blood tests for sexually transmitted diseases

11. complains about previous wives or girlfriends (it's the complainers who ruin relationships)

Lynn is a forty-four-year-old triage nurse in a busy city hospital. She and her physician husband have three young daughters. Both come from intact families of origin, although of different religious upbringings.

Lynn's acceptance criteria:

1. family-oriented and wants to have children

2. kind to everyone

3. has a sense of humor

4. has sensitivity for other people

5. loyal and dependable

6. intelligent

7. has the ability to provide finances so mom can stay home with the kids if she wants to

8. handy and helpful at home and without gender role definition

9. adventurous and wanting to try different things

10. never been married before

LYNN'S REJECTION CRITERIA:

1. more than one previous marriage

2. lied once (about anything at all)

3. trying to rush the different stages of the relationship, like engagement or a marriage

4. alcohol or drug problem of any kind (too difficult to reform)

5. not educated

6. does not have a job

7. says he will change for the better once he is married

Lynn's advice is to marry someone who hasn't been married before because that makes married life easier. She advises against living together before marriage because it robs the couple of the joy of moving into their first house together after they are married. The joy is the shared experience of deciding how your first marital household will be structured and decorated. If not done this way, one of the parties is moving into someone's already established turf, and eventually there will be conflict.

Lilo and Fritz* are in their seventies. They met and married in Germany, emigrated to the US, and settled in New England. Fritz worked as an engineer. Lilo is a housewife, landscaper, and manager of their properties. They have two grown and married children and five grandchildren. They offer the following screening criteria. Fritz says if you can answer yes to the following questions about a person, your marriage to that person has a good chance of working out.

Their acceptance criteria are:

1. Realize that you marry both the person and his or her clan. Can you put up with the clan?

2. Do you have an attraction, a spark for the other person?

3. Is the person wise with money? Did he or she work to better him or herself?

4. Does the person have a good work ethic, is willing to work and solve problems?

5. Are the person's political affiliation and views compatible with your own?

6. Do you realize that people do not change drastically? Do you accept and love the person as he or she is?

7. Is the person willing to learn, take advice, and be open-minded and appreciative?

8. Is the person intellectually compatible with you?

9. Check out the person's drinking. Are you all right with his or her alcohol consumption?

10. Look at the condition of the person's car. Is it in good condition? Is it clean?

11. Is this a person who increases your own feeling of financial security?

12. Is the person of good mental and physical health?

Ann* is a sixty-six-year-old retired clinical psychologist active in community groups promoting city improvement. She is close to her large extended family. Ann put herself through graduate school and never married, although she had opportunities to do so. Ann devoted her professional life to counseling young adults.

ANN'S ACCEPTANCE CRITERIA:

1. has similar values regarding concern for others

2. has the capacity to understand where the other person is coming from, i.e. is not closed-minded

3. has similar views on financial priorities

4. has similar views regarding education and religious values

5. is in agreement on whether or not to have children and how to raise them regarding career/family issues for both husband and wife

6. has similar attitudes about pleasure and its benefits in sexual, material, or emotional areas

Tom is a sixty-six-year-old engineer. His prior careers include professional ice hockey player, army officer and helicopter pilot, and statistical engineer for a private company. He is the youngest of nine children and is close to his large extended family. He has been married to his wife for thirty-five years and has three grown children.

TOM'S ACCEPTANCE CRITERIA:

1. have good family upbringing

2. intelligence has to be comparable or better

3. could complement my weaknesses

4. have common or similar values

5. willingness to have and raise children

6. similar religion or religious upbringing

7. be someone I can have mutual respect with

8. be hard working

9. takes reasonable care of herself in terms of appearance

10. is of similar age and is willing to try different things

Tom's rejection criteria:

1. an addict of some kind (shopping, gambling, drugs)

2. pregnant with someone else's child

3. has kids or was married before and hid it or lied about it

4. terminal disease

5. some reason why the person cannot have children or does not want children

6. any surprise discovery about the person

7. person is not a Christian

Tom's advice is that if you find that a person concealed or lied about having been married before, having children or abortions, then you should run away even if your wedding to this person is only two weeks away. S/he has too many problems, including being dishonest.

Edna is a seventy-two-year-old retired nurse. Her husband worked for the telephone company and died in an accident twenty-one years ago. Edna never remarried and has three grown children and five grandchildren.

Edna's acceptance criteria:

1. has a sense of humor and is able to see humor in situations, including in being poor

2. kind and loving

3. respectful of me and others

4. is honest and has integrity

5. loves family and wants children

6. is dependable

7. is handy and is able to build and fix things

8. we share a similar outlook on politics and life philosophies

9. is intelligent, can carry on a conversation, keeps up with the news, and is aware of what's going on in the world

10. someone who does not mind going to work every day

11. someone I have known for a long time, someone whose upbringing I understand, someone who has good values and *would not live with me* before marriage

Edna's Rejection Criteria:

1. an uninteresting person

2. someone having "not a bit of wit"

3. is self-absorbed and talks only of his job, goals, likes, and dislikes

4. is unable to connect with other people

Donald* is sixty-eight-years-old and has been married to his wife for several decades. One of his grown daughters is a licensed independent clinical social worker.

DONALD'S ACCEPTANCE CRITERIA:

1. is able to listen to partner's ideas

2. is able to agree to disagree

3. tries to be a good friend to my friends

4. is able to share in my interests

5. makes purchases that are sensible and beneficial to both of us

6. surprises me with things that are wanted but least expected

7. keeps personal life interesting

8. helps around the house because she wants to

9. enjoys taking vacations with me

Christopher is a fifty-seven-year-old Protestant clergyman who enjoys relating to his parishioners. He has administered to thousands of people in spiritual and physical need. Married to his wife of twenty-five years, he helped to raise his wife's three daughters from her former marriage to an alcoholic.

CHRISTOPHER'S ACCEPTANCE CRITERIA:

1. commitment to the Christian faith and the Lutheran church in particular

2. enthusiasm but not a compulsion for a neat living environment

3. a parallel enthusiasm for intimacy, compatible libido

4. she does not have to think like me, but she should love thinking and be good at it

5. a similar commitment to X number of children and to rearing them with a partner

6. energy for working and valuing work as important, for the enrichment of the life of others and oneself

7. having a capacity for laughter, a recognition that life is serious but not that serious

Christopher's rejection criteria:

1. a person without faith/belief or attention to the relationship of the human and the divine

2. untreated addictions—people who need to be in treatment ought to not marry until they get treatment and are in recovery

Doris is a fifty-seven-year-old health care researcher. Her first marriage to an alcoholic ended in divorce. Doris eventually married Christopher, and together they raised Doris's three daughters from her first marriage.

Doris' acceptance criteria:

1. a sense of humor and a joy in life

2. honesty and high values

3. common goals and beliefs

4. compassion and empathy

5. gentleness

6. a belief in marriage as a partnership, each giving to the other and sharing responsibilities and tasks

7. a deep love and attraction

8. similar interests but willingness to embrace each other's love of different arts

9. shared religious beliefs and faith life

10. commitment to families and each other's parents and children

DORIS'S REJECTION CRITERIA:

1. alcohol or drug problem

2. selfishness, self-absorption

3. lack of compassion

4. lack of respect for me and inability to value my opinion

5. inability to recognize my strengths and support me

6. unwillingness to share responsibilities, childcare, family, home tasks

7. stinginess

8. bad temper, uncontrolled anger

9. inability to express and communicate thoughts and feelings

10. mean spiritedness

Diane is sixty-seven years old and has been married to her husband for forty-seven years. Together they raised seven children, who are all grown with fifteen children between them. All are practicing Roman Catholics. While raising the children, Diane held part-time jobs. Her husband, George, worked as an engineer before his retirement. None of Diane's children are divorced. Diane herself came from a divorced home and wanted me to specifically state that she attributes the success of her marriage to her husband's characteristics, which he learned in his family of origin.

Diane's acceptance criteria:

1. loyalty to family—if there's loyalty to family of origin, there will be for wife and children

2. honesty in everything, especially if it is a painful subject

3. raised in a close family, in a pleasant atmosphere, with everyone on speaking terms

4. will treat me with the utmost respect

5. strength of character—knowing what he wants and acting on it

6. patience—lots of patience with people, with work, with assignments, with life

7. ability to concentrate on tasks, deliver good products, do quality work

8. supportive of children coming along, even though finances are very tight

9. can demonstrate love in different ways (it is okay to be reserved in public)

10. good morality and strong faith

E'S REJECTION CRITERIA:

1. the person never asks about me, my family, or friends

2. the person never puts out a cent for me but lets me treat him

3. his first priority is sexual

4. shows interest in unhealthy sex

5. is secretive

6. does not treat a woman like a lady

7. abnormal personal appearance reflecting the wrong values and disrespect for a person's body

8. cannot seem to make independent decisions

Jan is seventy-one years old. She and her husband have been married for fifty years and raised four children. Jan's husband worked as a surveyor and she as a bookkeeper. Jan's children are grown with children of their own. None are divorced.

JAN'S ACCEPTANCE CRITERIA:

1. a mature person, one who is able to make intelligent decisions

2. has family support from siblings and parents

3. appears trustworthy and honest

4. is considerate of my feelings, and the difference of opinion we may have

5. is a forgiving person, someone who can let things go

6. is willing to share in my interests and participate in activities to accommodate me

7. has similar values about the management of money

8. is able to share in the raising of children emotionally and physically

9. of same religion or of a religion compatible with mine

10. shares values in general and is in agreement on what is most important in life

Jan's advice concerning religious practice is to clarify ahead of time the role that religion will play in your lives and how you raise your children.

Jan's Rejection Criteria:

1. not of good moral standing

2. seems like a selfish person

3. has some kind of criminal background

4. boastful, talks big

5. someone who's way too clean or way too much of a slob

6. disagreement on whether he wants children

7. big difference in socioeconomic status

Lastly, I would like to offer my criteria:

1. mental stability

2. an active and bright intellect coupled with a strong work ethic that produces tangible achievements

3. must have good morals, including a natural kindness

4. good physical health and strength

5. strong desire to have a family and able to provide nurture and sacrifice for them

6. places similar emphasis on the importance of the children's religious upbringing and education

7. reasonably pleasant appearance and makes reasonable effort to look presentable

8. good credit history and wise with money

9. has ability to screen what he thinks before he says it

10. speech is tailored to and appropriate for the occasion

11. no history of lawsuits, frequent job changes, or dishonorable discharge from the military

My rejection criteria:

1. disagreement on politics and lack of knowledge about current events and politics

2. seems like a self-centered person

3. would not make a good father, does not like his parents, or is not relaxed around children

4. poor with money, is always short of money, is behind on bills, etc.

5. does not think before talking, especially in social situations

6. poor physical condition—this indicates a lack of self-discipline

7. too attractive physically

This last rejection criterion requires an explanation. I feel that being too attractive is a disadvantage because good-looking children and adults often receive undeserved preferential treatment because of their looks. As a consequence, very attractive people learn that their looks will get them anything and learn to place a disproportionate emphasis on their appearance and that of their companions. Because of the overemphasis on appearance, very attractive people often grow up without having built the inner core values of self-esteem, integrity, depth of thinking, and personal honesty necessary to a healthy life. If a person has poorly developed inner core values, they are very poorly suited for marriage. Also, physically attractive people automatically attract too many members of the opposite sex, which often leads to marital problems.

Appendix B:

A Guide to the Types of Mental Health Professionals Who Provide Medication and Psychotherapy

There are many types of mental health providers. The array of professionals who practice clinical therapy and provide psychiatric medications have very different training and skill sets. Because this is often confusing, I am providing a brief summary of the licensed and legally recognized mental health professionals (as of 2008).

A doctor of medicine (M.D.) or doctor of osteopathy (D.O.) completes medical school as well as hospital internships and residencies, totaling about seven to eight years of graduate school work. These medical doctors may practice as internists, family physicians, obstetricians/gynecologists, and so forth. All medical doctors may do brief, informal psychotherapy, although most do not and are not trained in this specialty. All medical doctors can prescribe medicines to treat mental health disorders, although some are not comfortable doing so and refer to psychiatrists who are medical doctors who specialize in the treatment of mental health disorders with prescription drugs and/or psychotherapy. Most often, psychiatrists prescribe the needed medicine and refer the psychotherapy work to other mental health providers.

Other professionals who may legally prescribe psychiatric medications are specially trained psychiatric nurse practitioners and physician's assistants, most of whom work in medical offices and consult with medical doctors. Specially trained and certified psychologists may also prescribe psychiatric medicines in the states of Louisiana and New Mexico and in the armed forces.

A psychologist typically has doctor of philosophy (Ph.D.) or a doctorate in education (D. Ed.) degree. A psychologist completes three to seven years of graduate school, including supervised pre- and postdoctoral internships and also writes and defends a dissertation. The doctoral dissertation is an experimental study conducted during graduate school and evaluated by faculty members prior to granting the degree. The purpose of writing the dissertation is to educate the student in the systematic evaluation of information and research data (although of late, some graduate school faculties allow dissertations that are not of an experimental nature).

A psychologist may also have a doctor of psychology (Psy.D.) degree. This professional has three to five years of graduate school and a supervised internship but rarely writes and defends a dissertation.

Mental health professionals can have different master's degrees. The most common are M.S. (master of science in counseling, psychology, or related fields), M.A. (master of arts degree in psychology) or M.S.W. (master of social work). Once they work as licensed therapists, these professionals may have the following behind their names such as L.M.H.C (licensed mental health counselor) and L.I.C.S.W. (licensed independent clinical social worker). Master's level therapists typically have two years of graduate schoolwork, during which they practice psychotherapy under supervision and may be required to write and defend a master's thesis.

In addition to getting graduate degrees, all professionals who wish to do therapy with the public must obtain a license to practice from the State Board of Registry.

A license to practice is granted by the state in which the professional wishes to practice. Licensure procedures may differ by state. Generally, the individual has to be of good moral character, demonstrate competence in their field, have the prerequisite degrees and training, and then pass a licensing examination. The license has to be updated every few years.

The license to practice is a public and legal permit for a doctor or therapist to work with the public. Licenses continue to be regulated by the State Board and thus provide protection for the consumer. If a licensed provider violates the code of conduct or offers poor service, the State Board reviews complaints against the provider and determines the consequences.

Health insurance companies allow only licensed providers to serve their members and pay for services provided by their in-network providers.

Not everyone with a graduate school education is licensed to practice therapy or dispense medication, because not everyone applies to have a license or is not granted a license to practice.

Some people sidestep the licensure process and advertise their therapy services as life coaches, psychotherapists, hypnotists, addiction specialists, behavior modification specialists, or neuromuscular practitioners. While these individuals may have graduate degrees, there are no such licenses for these designations dispensed by the State Board of Registry. As such, the public has no legal recourse to any negligent action by unlicensed providers. The services of these persons are not reimbursed by health care insurance policies.

Many people are not aware that their health insurance policy may cover therapy visits to licensed providers. This is because most health insurance policies have separate medical and mental health benefits parts. The mental health benefits part may consist of another two parts: one set of benefits for the treatment of alcohol and drug issues, the other for mental health issues. If you want help for alcohol, drug, or mental health issues, it is likely that your health insurance will cover most of the cost if you select a licensed, in-network mental health provider. Contact your health insurance company to understand the benefits you are entitled to.

To find out who is licensed to practice therapy in your location, contact the Board of Registry of medical doctors, psychologists, licensed independent clinical social workers, or licensed mental health counselors (some other entities such as "family therapists" may be allowed to practice in your state as well). Licensed and registered mental health providers are able to participate and might be providers for your insurance plan. This means that if you receive psychotherapy or medication from one of them, your health insurance may cover some of the cost of your therapy visits or medications.

Another way to find a therapist or psychiatrist is to call your health insurance company. Most health insurance companies maintain a listing of in-network providers and their areas of special expertise. Your insurance company usually reimburses the work of in-network providers, although you may be responsible for co-payments, deductibles to your policy, and for obtaining authorization for services.

Endnotes

Chapter 1
Case Study and the Discussion of Common Myths

1   R. Kippen, B. Chapman, and P. Yu, "What's Love Got to Do with It?" (www.News-Medical.net July 16, 2009).

2   Ibid

D. Popenoe and D.B. Whitehead, "Should We Live Together? What Young Adults Need to Know about Cohabitation before Marriage. National Marriage Project: The Next Generation Series" January, 1999. (The National Marriage Project, Rutgers, the State University of New Jersey).

P.R. Amato, "Explaining the Intergenerational Transmission of Divorce" (*Journal of Marriage and Family* 58, 1966), 628-640.

D. DeVaus, L. Qu, and R. Weston, "Premarital Cohabitation and Subsequent Marital Instability" (*Family Matters* 65, 2003), 43-49.

B.E. Hohmann-Marriott, "Shared Beliefs and the Union Stability of Married and Cohabitating Couples" (*Journal of Marriage and Family* 68, 2006), 1015-1028.

J.D. Teachman, "Stability Across Cohorts in Divorce Risk Factors" (*Demography* 39, 2002), 331-351.

3   D. Popenoe and D.B. Whitehead, *Ten Important Research Findings on Marriage and Choosing a Marriage Partner: Helpful Facts for Young Adults. National Marriage Project: Ten Things to know Series* (Information Brief, November, 2004. The National Marriage Project Rutgers, the State University of New Jersey).

4   A. DeMaris and K Vaninadha Rao, "Premarital Cohabitation and Marital Instability in the United States: A Reassessment" (*Journal of Marriage and the Family* 54, 1992),178-190.

P.J. Smock, "Cohabitation in the United States: An Appraisal of Research Themes, Findings, and Implications" (*Annual Review of Sociology* 26, 2000), 1-20.

P.J. Smock, "Living Arrangements and Family Formation Attitudes in Early Adulthood" (*Journal of Marriage and Family* 59, 1997), 595-611.

S.L. Brown, "The Effect of Union Type on Psychological Well-Being: Depression Among Cohabitators Versus Marrieds" (*Journal of Health and Social Behavior* 41, 2002), 241-55.

C.L. Cohan and S. Kleinbaum, "Toward a Greater Understanding of the Cohabitation Effect: Premarital Cohabitation and Marital Communication" (*Journal of Marriage and the Family* 64 2002), 180-192.

Chapter 2

Thinking—the First Step in Marrying Well

5   U.S. Bureau of the Census, 1982.

6   Article in *USA Today*, June 1, 1999.

7   L. Harris, *Inside America* (Vintage Books, 1987).

8   G. Barna, *The Future of the American Family* (Chicago: Moody, 1993).

9   D. Hurley, "Divorce Rate: It's Not as High as You Think" (*The New York Times*, April 29, 2005).

10   D. Popenoe and D.B. Whitehead, *Ten Important Research Findings on Marriage and Choosing a Marriage Partner: Helpful Facts for Young Adults. National Marriage Project: Ten Things to Know Series* (Information Brief, November 2004. The National Marriage Project, the State University of New Jersey).

11   Ibid.

12   D. Popenoe and D.B. Whitehead, "Should We Live Together?" Ibid.

13   F. Alford-Cooper, *For Keeps: Marriages that Last a Lifetime* (Armonk, N:Y.: M.E. Sharpe, 1998).

J. Wallerstein, and S. Blakeslee, *The Good Marriage* (Boston: Houghton Mifflin, 1995).

R. Lauer, and J. Lauer, "Factors in Long-Term Marriage" (*Journal of Family Issues* 7, 1986), 382-390.

14   D. Popenoe and D.B. Whitehead, *Ten Important Research Findings on Marriage and Choosing a Marriage Partner: Helpful Facts for Young Adults. National Marriage Project: Ten Things to Know Series* (Information Brief, November 2004. The National Marriage Project, the State University of New Jersey).

15   F. Alford-Cooper, *For Keeps: Marriages that Last a Lifetime* (Armonk, N:Y.: M.E. Sharpe, 1998).

J. Wallerstein, and S. Blakeslee, *The Good Marriage* (Boston: Houghton Mifflin, 1995).

R. Lauer and J. Lauer, Ibid

Chapter 5
How to Tell if Someone is Lying and What to Do About It

16   D. Grubin, MD, "Getting at the Truth about Pathological Lying" (*Journal of the American Academy of Psychiatry and the Law Online* 33, 2005), 350-353.

17   S. Mann, A. Vrij, R. Bull, "Detecting True Lies: Police Offi-
      cers' Ability to Detect Suspects' Lies" (*Journal of Applied
      Psychology* 89, 2004), 137-49.

      P. Ekman, M. O'Sullivan, and M.G. Frank, "A Few Can
      Catch a Liar" (*Psychol Sci* 10, 1999), 263-6.

18   P. Ekman, Te*lling Lies* (New York: W.W. Norton, 1985).

19   C.C. Dike, M. Baranoski, and E.E.H. Griffith, "Pathologi-
      cal Lying Revisited" (J Am Acad Psychiatry Law 33, 2005),
      342-349.

      *Diagnostic and Statistical Manual of Mental Disorders
      (DSM –IV)*: American Psychiatric Association,1994.

20   B.H. King and C.V. Ford, "Pseudologia Fantascia" (*Acta
      Psychiatr Scand* 77, 1988), 1-6.

21   J.G. Modell, J.M. Mountz, and C.V. Ford, "Pathological
      Lying Associated with Thalamic Dysfunction Demon-
      strated by (99m/tc) HMPAO SPECT" (*Journal of Neuro-
      psychiatry* 4, 1992), 442-6.

      J.M. Nunez, B.J. Casey, T. Egner, T. Hare, and J. Hirsch,
      "Intentional False Responding Shares Neural Substrates with
      Response Conflict and Cognitive Control" (*Neuroimage* 25, 2005),
      267-277.

22   D.A. Kashy and B.M. De Paulo, "Who Lies?" (*Journal of
      Personal Social Psychology* 70, 1996), 1037-51.

23 C.C. Dike, M. Baranoski, and E.E.H. Griffith, "Pathological Lying Revisited" (J Am Acad Psychiatry Law 33, 2005), 342-349.

24 I am indebted to my son Tom for some of these ideas (private conversation).

listen|imagine|view|experience

AUDIO BOOK DOWNLOAD INCLUDED WITH THIS BOOK!

In your hands you hold a complete digital entertainment package. In addition to the paper version, you receive a free download of the audio version of this book. Simply use the code listed below when visiting our website. Once downloaded to your computer, you can listen to the book through your computer's speakers, burn it to an audio CD or save the file to your portable music device (such as Apple's popular iPod) and listen on the go!

How to get your free audio book digital download:

1. Visit www.tatepublishing.com and click on the e|LIVE logo on the home page.
2. Enter the following coupon code:
   b0c7-ed02-194e-ac78-d553-0a62-dd69-a9dc
3. Download the audio book from your e|LIVE digital locker and begin enjoying your new digital entertainment package today!